To Great Grandfa[ther]
in Celebrati[on]
Baptism of
Robert Dalton Rose
on
December 30, 2017
at
Blessed Sacrament Church
Stowe, Vermont

PAINTING ON LIGHT

A RESTORATION

The Story of André Girard's
Dramatic Windows and Murals
at Blessed Sacrament Catholic Church
Stowe, Vermont

Professor Josephine Belloso

Painting on Light: A Restoration— The Story of André Girard's
Dramatic Windows and Murals at Blessed Sacrament Catholic Church

Copyright © 2017, Blessed Sacrament Catholic Church, Stowe, Vermont

ISBN: 978-0-9995393-0-9
Cataloging in Publication data block and Library of Congress Control Number
information available for this title upon request.

Front Cover:
Detail of The Transfiguration Window
Back Cover:
A Watercolor Painting of Blessed Sacrament Church
by Mary Chambers

Book Design and Layout
Josephine Belloso

For more information and to purchase additional copies,
please contact Blessed Sacrament Church at www.PaintingOnLight.com

Printed in Canada

Restoration of the Sacred

The poet Dante wrote that "Beauty awakens the soul to act." The Church has

consistently taught that encountering true beauty is a way of coming to know the

source of all beauty—God. For two thousand years, Christian artists have shared in

God's creative work by allowing something of the beauty of God to be seen in their

works of art. Entering Blessed Sacrament Church, which is the "Domus Dei"—

the House of God—the soul is awakened by the work of the artist André Girard;

awakened to prayer, praise and thanksgiving. For all who have contributed

to the restoration of this beautiful House of God, we give great thanks.

From Fr. Benedict Kiely

Pastor of Blessed Sacrament Catholic Church

Father Benedict Kiely's term as Pastor of Blessed Sacrament Church ended in July 2016. Like Brother Joseph Dutton, he has answered the call to minister to the suffering and disadvantaged of this world. His next mission will be to help the persecuted and displaced Christians from Iraq and Syria through his charity Nasarean.org.

Author's Note

St. Damien, born Joseph DeVeuster, is referred to as Father Damien throughout this book in order to keep to the historical context of the time, when he was a simple priest struggling to get help from civic as well as Church authorities to improve the conditions of the leper colony in Molokai.

The term leprosy instead of Hansen's Disease is also used in a historical context to better understand the suffering of those afflicted with this disfiguring disease at the time, and also to explain the reasoning behind the need to isolate those having the disease from the rest of society.

DEDICATION

*Brother
Joseph Dutton*

*André Girard
Artist*

*Father
Damien DeVeuster*

This book is dedicated to Blessed Sacrament Church and the three men whose remarkable lives were so important to its heritage and mission.

First, to Brother Joseph Dutton, beloved son of Stowe, whose heroic service to humanity is exemplified by the 45 years he devoted to caring for the lepers at the settlement on the island of Molokai in Hawaii.

Secondly, to Father Damien, whose dedicated life bringing spiritual healing and hope to those afflicted with leprosy in Molokai served as an inspiration for Joseph Dutton to follow his example. The Belgian priest, who eventually became a leper himself, literally sacrificed his own life in serving his flock. He was canonized a Saint by Pope Benedict XVI in 2009.

And lastly, this book is dedicated to André Girard, a world-renowned liturgical artist who was so moved by the selfless dedication of Brother Dutton and Father Damien that he retold their story on large-scale murals surrounding Blessed Sacrament Church so others might be inspired by their lives of service to those in need.

Sister Jean Dominici DeMaria, OP, PhD

The contents of this book were organized and processed
by Sister Jean Dominici DeMaria, OP, PhD.
It was composed in Adobe Creative Cloud software—
Photoshop, InDesign, and Illustrator,
using Adobe Garamond.

ACKNOWLEDGMENTS

I wish to express my appreciation to the Pastor of Blessed Sacrament Church, Father Benedict Kiely and the Restoration Committee under the leadership of Jim Brochhausen, for their support and encouragement during the writing of this book. My thanks are also extended to Lynn Altadonna for his dedication and assistance in the planning and execution of this endeavor.

Most especially, I wish to acknowledge my debt to Sr. Jean Dominici DeMaria, OP, PhD, for her expertise and collaboration which not only facilitated the digital restoration of the windows, but also the digital processing of this book for publication.

My gratitude is also expressed to Mary Chambers, a former parishioner, for the use of her watercolor painting of Blessed Sacrament Church on the back cover of this book.

My thanks are also given to John LaPan for his successful coordination and direction of local craftsmen in the installation of the newly restored windows at Blessed Sacrament Church.

Lastly, I wish to thank my niece, Jeanne McMurray, for her valuable assistance and advice throughout the preparation of the book.

Detail from a Window with Angels

TABLE OF CONTENTS

Painting on Light

*"I came into the world as light
so that everyone who believes in me
might not remain in darkness."*

—JOHN 12:46

Memorial Plaque
at the entrance to Blessed Sacrament Catholic Church

A History of
Blessed Sacrament Catholic Church

Stowe, Vermont 1949

Blessed Sacrament Church has a unique and extraordinary history. Its humble beginnings started with a small congregation which gathered on Sundays in the basement of the Town Hall of Stowe to attend Mass, because they did not have a church building of their own. In 1947 when Bishop Ryan assigned Rev. Francis E. McDonough to be Pastor of The Holy Cross Church in Morrisville, he also asked him to be Pastor of the Stowe Parish and to eventually build a church for their small congregation.

Much earlier the Knights of Columbus had planned to build a church in Stowe that was to honor the memory of Brother Joseph Dutton. The 19th Century Stowe native was remembered and admired for his work with Father Damien (who is now St. Damien), in caring for the lepers on the island of Molokai. Although the new church was to be dedicated to The Blessed Sacrament, it was decided to fulfill the earlier plans of the Knights

by having the church also serve as a memorial to Br. Joseph Dutton.

After several unsuccessful attempts to find a suitable property on which to build the church, Fr. McDonough thought he had found the perfect site. Although the property was not for sale, Fr. McDonough approached the owner about the possibility of selling a portion of his land as a location for a church. The owner, Mr. McCutcheon, said he might consider it, but would have to think about it. After several days, Fr. McDonough again spoke with the owner, and happened to mention that the church was to be built in the memory of Br. Joseph Dutton. Mr. McCutcheon's reply surprised Fr. McDonough. "Well," he said to the Pastor, "that's interesting. You know he was born in the house I live in and my grandmother was a younger sister of his grandmother."[1]

In Fr. McDonough's remembrances of the building of Blessed Sacrament Church, he expressed his own reaction to this astounding coincidence as follows: "Well, if the Angel Gabriel had appeared to me on the spot, and said this was the place to build a church, I couldn't have been more sure of it."[2]

It was with great enthusiasm that Fr. McDonough visited Maria von Trapp and her family to ask for their prayers for the success of his efforts to acquire the property. However, when the Pastor presented the offer to Bishop Ryan, the Bishop did not consider the property to be a suitable site. Feeling completely frustrated, Fr. McDonough reported the Bishop's response to Maria von Trapp, who offered to speak with the Bishop the very next morning. Mrs. von Trapp's powers of persuasion must have been considerable, because by the afternoon of that same day the Bishop had approved the purchase of the property, and directed Fr. McDonough to start building the church. On November 2, 1948 Fr. McDonough had the satisfaction of turning the first sod for the construction of Blessed Sacrament Church.

Since winter was approaching, construction on the church was immediately begun. The architectural firm of Wittier and Goodrich from Burlington, Vermont designed a rustic church suited to the needs of its small congregation and characterized by its simplicity and harmonious proportions. Local natural materials were used such as basic pine panels for the walls of the church, and green Vermont marble for the floors with the sanctuary space being done in red marble.

After receiving permission from Bishop Ryan, Fr. McDonough was finally able to say the first Mass for the congregation in their own church. The Trapp Family Singers returned from a tour in England to sing at this special Mass. Fr. McDonough described this day as "a glorious occasion".[3]

The church was officially dedicated with the title Blessed Sacrament Catholic Church on March 6, 1949 by His Excellency Most Rev. Edward F. Ryan, D.D., Bishop of Burlington. The feast of Corpus Christi, the official feast of the Blessed Sacrament, was celebrated by Bishop Ryan on June 16th. This was the official public dedication of the Church. In his remembrances Father McDonough describes it as, ". . . a beautiful day, the Trapps sang the *Missa Brevis* by Mozart. It was absolutely magnificent."[4]

Before making any specific plans for the decoration of the church, Fr. McDonough decided to consult with Maurice Lavanoux, who was a personal friend and the Editor of *Liturgical Arts Quarterly Magazine*. Father received more than the expert advice he had sought. Mr. Lavanoux spoke to him about the possibility of receiving a set of 14 paintings of the *Way of the Cross* which Mr. Otto Spaethe had commissioned to be donated to a new church. The 14 *Stations of the Cross* had been painted by the French liturgical artist, André Girard.

Several months later, Fr. McDonough was pleasantly surprised to receive a visit from not only Maurice Lavanoux, but Mr. and Mrs. Otto Spaethe and the artist, André Girard. They had all come to see if it was a suitable site for the commissioned paintings. Within a few days, Maurice Lavanoux was able to give Fr. McDonough the good news that the *Stations of the Cross* were to be donated to Blessed Sacrament Church. He also reported that the artist, André Girard, had expressed the desire to decorate the entire church. Since the parish had very limited funds, Mr. Girard had said he would be willing to do the work if he would be provided the necessary art materials and lodging for himself and his family.

The fourteen paintings making up the *Way of the Cross* that André Girard had painted for Mr. and Mrs. Spaethe measured two feet square and were well suited in scale to the proportions of the church. However, Girard's interpretation of the suffering of Christ as He struggled on the way to Calvary was very moving. His dramatic use of color and light as well as the beauty of each painting created an impact that was far beyond their size. Girard, like Rembrandt, also effectively employed the chiaroscuro technique, which utilizes a darkened setting for a scene and bathes the main action with a glowing light. This creates an atmosphere of drama and mystery through which we are drawn into each scene to more completely understand what is taking place. As we follow each painting we begin to have a sense of experiencing the events of Christ's journey to His crucifixion and death. Nine of the original fourteen paintings are reproduced on the facing page.

The triptych André Girard created for Blessed Sacrament Church was highly personalized. It is presently located on the wall to the right of the altar. Traditionally, triptychs have three panels with the central panel having a formal image of Christ or

Jesus Is Condemned to Death

Jesus Bears His Cross

Jesus Falls the First Time

The Way of the Cross

Jesus Is Helped by Simon

Jesus Meets His Mother

Veronica Wipes the Face of Jesus

Jesus Dies on the Cross

Jesus Is Taken Down from the Cross

Jesus Is Laid in the Tomb

The Triptych of Our Lady of Stowe

the Madonna in a historic or ethereal setting. What makes Girard's triptych unique is that the central panel portrays Joseph, Mary, and the Infant Jesus in a Vermont setting with a recognizable image of Blessed Sacrament Church in the distance. It is referred to as *Our Lady of Stowe*. The panel to the left portrays a series of homey and informal scenes of the early life of Christ. Mary is first shown caring for the baby Christ, then walking with the growing child, teaching Him and also playing with Him. They are scenes that any contemporary mother and child can identify with. The

right panel is more traditional, in that it depicts Christ's Public Life, Passion, and Death. Although the triptych is a small-scaled work, it encompasses the total life of Christ in a fresh, new, and engaging manner.

One of André Girard's most important works in Blessed Sacrament Church is sometimes not noticed by visitors. It is the large-scaled oil painting on stretched canvas that covers the wall behind the altar. This piece presents a significant and appropriate setting for the services that take place there, which include the consecration of the Blessed Sacrament at

Angels and Arabesques decorate the ceiling

The Altarpiece depicting the Communion of Saints

Mass. The focal point of the painting centers on the images of the Father, Son and the Holy Spirit, which provide a visual manifestation of the Triune God, and is a specific reminder of the Divine Presence in the church.

André Girard designed the altarpiece to express the concept of the Communion of Saints, which in the Catholic Church signifies the union with God, the blessed in heaven and His people on earth. Therefore the painting encompasses the settings of the heavens and the earth. In the upper section the images of the angels, painted in tones of gold and bronze, become somewhat ethereal as they are bathed in a radiance of light emanating from the sacred figures. The painting has such an overall effect of light, that for those who choose to use it as an inspiration during Mass, the images can reinforce what is taking place. However, the painting is so slight in its definition that it would not be a distraction for those who choose not to focus on it. The lower portion of the painting represents the people on earth looking upward to the heavens.

The faces of angelic hosts are continued following a panel to the side of the altar and extending from there to the entire church, serving as a unifying element behind the *Stations of the Cross*, and giving them a sense

Father Benedict Kiely Raising the Chalice during the Consecration

of movement and connection. Looking upward at the ceiling, angelic faces again provide a subtle continuity to Girard's overall church decoration.

Although it was his paintings of *The Way of the Cross* that brought André Girard to Blessed Sacrament Church, it was upon seeing these small works in this empty rustic space that set Girard's creative mind

The Annunciation

The Nativity

Jesus among the Doctors

soaring. He began to envision how he might decorate the entire church with his paintings, an opportunity given to very few artists.

Fr. McDonough remembers that when Girard first visited Blessed Sacrament Church, he kept looking at the windows and saying "C'est magnifique!"[5] The Pastor wondered why Girard considered these ordinary windows to be so special, but Girard's artistic mind was actually envisioning what a magnificent opportunity they would provide for his illustrations of the life of Christ in the innovative painting technique he had developed which he called "Painting on Light." Using this technique Girard would paint on the clear glass against the light of the sun passing through the windows. Juxtaposing translucent and opaque paint in multiple layers, Girard could create subtle as well as dramatic effects.

André Girard was artistically and emotionally inspired when he learned about the life of Br. Joseph Dutton. Instead of doing a singular static portrait of him as might have been expected, Girard decided to illustrate his story by painting twelve large-scale murals in black on the exterior walls of the church. The murals begin with his arrival in Molokai, and end with the salute to Br. Dutton by the American battleships sent to Molokai on the specific orders of President Theodore Roosevelt. A viewing of these murals is to witness Br. Dutton's life and dedication.

In 1974 Blessed Sacrament Church realized André Girard's paintings on the windows as well as the exterior murals were deteriorating due to the constant exposure to Vermont's extreme weather conditions. If left untended, they might be lost forever. Josephine Belloso, who had studied with Girard, was selected to do the restorations. During two summers, she restored the windows, the exterior murals, the doors, and the pediment.

Twenty years later, the exterior panels again needed restoration which was done by Wolfgang P. Kier.

In 2005 a major expansion of Blessed Sacrament Church was undertaken. A Parish Center was constructed, and a narthex or vestibule, was added to the entrance to the church. In addition to this, the expansion of the nave with a transept provided fifty percent more space for those attending services. In 2010 André Girard's artwork again required restoration. Matthew

H. Strong, a local artist, restored Girard's paintings of the exterior murals, the doors, and the pediment.

Unfortunately, the paintings on the windows were so dried out, that they could no longer continue to be restored by repainting. However, Josephine Belloso re-created the paintings in collaboration with Sr. Jean Dominici, by digitally restoring photographs of the windows. These digital images were then printed on special vinyl and attached to a new set of windows. The replacement of Girard's original artwork was a tremendous loss, but the eventual deterioration of his extraordinary imagery would have been a tragedy. This digital process, introduced by Miss Belloso, ensured that André Girard's window illuminations would remain permanent images, and never have to be restored again.

It is extremely rare that a single artist has been given the opportunity to decorate an entire church. During Medieval times, churches were decorated by hundreds of artisans over generations. Even Michelangelo in the Renaissance did not decorate the entire Sistine Chapel. So André Girard truly experienced a unique opportunity to develop and express the spirited character of Blessed Sacrament Church through his art.

The artistry of André Girard is an integral part of the history of Stowe, as well as of Blessed Sacrament Church. An internationally acclaimed artist, he gifted this small town and this small church with a treasure of his creation. His artistic vision encompassed not only the religious aspect of his subject matter, but was also sensitive to Stowe's heritage in commemorating the life of a most important native son in an exceptional manner.

He also respected the natural rustic aspect of the environment and made use of the natural wood walls of the church as the background for the Dutton murals. He incorporated the setting of Vermont for a painting of the Holy Family, and embraced the natural daylight into his window illuminations. Thus, Blessed Sacrament Church reflects an important part of Stowe's history. It is a unique church that provides a place of respite to reflect not only on the beauty of Girard's paintings, but also on the lives that inspired them.

The congregation of Blessed Sacrament Church is comprised of about 200 families, but the church's daily attendance is increased by the many visitors who travel to Stowe throughout the year to enjoy its many offerings.

Brother Dutton Takes Over Additional Responsibiities

The Distribution of Holy Communion

Father Damien in the Confessional

Brother Joseph Dutton

Beloved Son of Stowe
1843–1931

Stowe, Vermont can take pride in being the birthplace of Brother Joseph Dutton. A selfless humanitarian, Dutton's devotion to the care of the lepers in Molokai for more than four decades inspired people throughout the world during his lifetime. Born Ira Dutton on April 27, 1843, he spent the first four years of his life on the family farm in Stowe which providentially, over one hundred years later, became the building site for Blessed Sacrament Church.

In 1847, Ira's father, seeking better business opportunities, moved the family to Janesville, Wisconsin. Ira's mother, who was a schoolteacher, decided to homeschool her child. Although he resisted going to a regular academy at age twelve, he proved to be an intelligent and industrious student. Finalizing his years at Milton Academy, he then took on various jobs to pay for his continuing education at Milton College.

Soon after the outbreak of The Civil War, Ira Dutton and his friends joined the military on the side of The North. He was soon appointed Regimental Quartermaster Sergeant, a position which kept him from taking part in any battles, but gave him experience in planning and ordering supplies for the needs of the troops as well as for the construction of camps and the building of bridges. After the war ended, Ira Dutton married a young woman he had met briefly during his military service. Unfortunately, she left him within a year and asked for a divorce.

Ira became extremely disillusioned by this event because he had truly loved her and had taken his marriage vows seriously. This disappointing incident, plus the nature of the new job he had taken on with the army, created a very depressing period in his life. His position involved disinterring the bodies of The Civil War dead from the battlefields, and bringing them to be buried in the new national cemeteries. As a result of his personal and professional experiences during this time, Ira Dutton began drinking to forget the loss of his wife, and the horrors he had to face each day disenterring the war dead. Although Dutton continued

Ira B. Dutton in his Civil War uniform

to drink for about ten years, he made a serious effort to remain sober during the day. In this way, his drinking did not interfere with fulfilling his work-related responsibilities.

Finally, Ira Dutton realized his dependence on liquor was destroying his life. In 1876, The centennial year of the signing of the Declaration of Independence, he declared his own independence from liquor and began facing a new future. His resolve was complete. He not only stopped drinking, but also felt a strong responsibility to make amends to God for past transgressions. After considering several religions, he decided to become a Catholic, and when baptized, he took on a new name, Joseph, to begin his new life.

Seeking to find peace and put his life in order, Ira, now Joseph, joined the Trappist Monks in a monastery called Gethsemani in Kentucky. The regimented life of the monastery was not unlike the life Dutton had experienced during his military service. The hard work, silence, and periods of prayer, offered him a wonderful opportunity for reflection on what he should do with his life. Joseph Dutton never took formal vows. After twenty months, he realized that he wanted to lead a penitential life serving God through the serving of others, rather than the reclusive life of prayer and meditation. And so, he left the monastery.

While attending a religious conference, Dutton read an article about Father Damien, a Belgian priest, who had devoted his life ministering to the lepers in Molokai and who had now become a victim of the

Gethsemani Monastery

Father Damien with a few choir members

disease himself. Dutton immediately decided this was the perfect way he could live a life of penance and spend his life serving others. He began to make arrangements to go to Molokai to assist Father Damien in his work. As soon as he acquired the documentation and received all the necessary permissions from the Church as well as the civil authorities, he set out for Molokai. The only thing he neglected to do was to notify Father Damien he was coming!

On July 19, 1886, Father Damien went to the boat landing at Kalaupapa. He was in his buggy, drawn by a gentle old horse named Daisy, expecting to receive new patients who had been exiled by the government and forced to leave their homes and families. It was Father Damien's habit to meet the new arrivals, because he realized these patients probably felt rejected and isolated by all of society. Through the greeting of each one personally, he hoped they would know that he welcomed them and would take care of them.

However, an unexpected passenger arrived who was not part of the group of lepers. Joseph Dutton, wearing a denim suit which gave him a somewhat of a military bearing looked around. He soon noticed Father Damien seated in his buggy and in his usual priestly cassock and straw hat. Dutton immediately introduced himself, and declared he had come to devote himself for the rest of his life to help Father Damien in his work. Father Damien must have felt heaven finally answered his prayers, because he had frequently petitioned the

government as well as the church authorities, and God Himself, to send him priests, brothers and sisters, to assist him in his labors. A few volunteers had come, but stayed briefly. Father Damien must have felt great joy. Here at last was someone to share his burdens. Although Joseph Dutton was not part of a religious community, from that moment on, Father Damien referred to Joseph Dutton as Brother Joseph.

Father Damien was so encouraged by Brother Joseph's arrival, he immediately began building a small one-room cottage for him. This was later expanded to two rooms in order to include an office, but it was the place where Brother Dutton lived during his years at the leper Settlement. The day after his arrival, Dutton was ready to begin his new life of service. He consulted Doctor Arthur Mouritz, the medical superintendent of the Colony, to ask for instructions on the correct way to cleanse and bandage the sores of the colonists. This was an intimidating task because of the strong possibility of contamination and the distasteful aspect of the sores. However, Dutton's experience after The Civil War, picking up the bodies of the fallen soldiers, had given him the moral strength and courage to face the pain, suffering, and deformities experienced by the patients.

Father Damien and Brother Dutton were quite different in personality, appearance, and character. However, they developed a deep friendship and bonded

Brother Joseph with Father Damien's horse, Daisy

Brother Dutton in front of his cottage

together since they shared a common goal. Very often in the evening they would meet and walk together to exchange ideas and process the events of their day. It was also a time to possibly discuss problems or plans for the future.

Brother Dutton was a tireless and dedicated worker. Aside from attending to the personal needs of the lepers, he was put in charge of the care and maintenance of two churches. After completing his own duties, Brother Dutton generously did all that he could to assist Father Damien in his work.

Father Damien was very pleased with his new assistant, and described him to a friend as, ". . . a middle-aged, well educated man. He resides here with me and as a true brother helps me caring for the sick. He too, though not a priest, finds his comfort in the Blessed Sacrament. You will admire with me the almighty power of grace in favor of my new companion."[6]

Father Damien was aware that as the illness of his leprosy advanced, his days on earth were numbered. However, instead of slowing down, the possibility that Brother Dutton could help him fulfill his dreams for the Colony motivated him to start many new projects. These were undertakings he would probably be unable to complete, but would be left to the reliable and willing Dutton to finish.

One of the many frustrations that Father Damien had suffered in Molokai was that he didn't have priests, brothers or sisters to give him the spiritual support he needed. Before his death, for a short time, he had the consolation of three priests and several brothers

and sisters who were finally assigned to help him with his work at the Settlement. Father Damien died on April 15, 1889. After nearly 16 years of ministering to the afflicted lepers at the Settlement, his death at the age of 49 was mourned not only by the people at the Colony who lost their pastor, their teacher, and their closest and most-beloved friend, but also by the whole world. People everywhere had been very moved when it had been discovered Father Damien had contracted leprosy himself but still continued to work taking care of his flock. It was felt he had literally sacrificed his very life for them.

Father Damien once explained to a visitor that funeral ceremonies at the Colony were opportunities for celebration. The church band and choir used on feast days were also used at funerals, because he wanted the ceremonies to celebrate the life of those who died and give them a joyous send-off.[7]

Now it was the time to celebrate Father Damien's life. On April 18, 1889, a High Requiem Mass was said for him at the Church of Saint Philomena. Afterward, the church band led what was probably the entire Molokai population and visitors in procession to the cemetery. All took part in celebrating Father Damien's life, but were saddened they would forever miss his loving and inspiring presence in their lives.

After the death of Father Damien, the awesome responsibility of directing the Settlement fell on Brother Dutton. Fortunately, his position as Regimental Quartermaster in the service had given him experience in estimating needs for both food supplies as well as construction and maintenance needs.

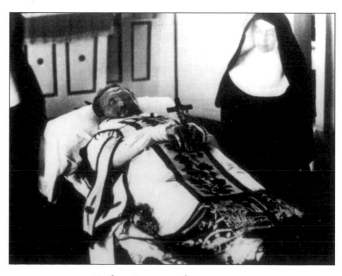

Father Damien lying in state

Brother Dutton with the boys of the Baldwin Home

Among the first building projects Brother Dutton wished to attend to, was the reconstruction of the Church of St. Philomena. This was a church that had been so closely associated with Father Damien that it had been called Damien's Church. Damaged by a storm in the past, it was now in need of expansion to accommodate the greater number of parishioners. Father Damien had dreamed of fully reconstructing and expanding it. This was the place where Brother Dutton and Father Damien had spent many hours in prayer, adoration and worship. It gave Brother Dutton great satisfaction to complete the rebuilding of this church, because it was a promise he fulfilled to his friend and spiritual companion.

A new residence for the orphan boys, ages eight to eighteen, was also an important project for Brother Dutton. The original residence was no longer adequate, because the Settlement was receiving many more youths than it had before. Named The Baldwin Home in honor of its principle donor, Henry P. Baldwin, it consisted of forty-five cottages arranged in a quadrangle around a central courtyard.

Although Brother Dutton was in charge of running the residence, as the number of boys increased, he was given some assistants. Among them was another Belgian priest, Fr. Lambert Carmardy, who had led an adventurous life. Having served initially in southern India, he was later assigned to an American Indian Reservation in Oregon. Father Carmardy probably

kept the boys entertained with stories of what it was like to live in the wild west with cowboys and Indians, wolves and wildcats. He must also have been a welcome companion to Brother Dutton, who had so much pride in his homeland.

In 1898, the United States government formally annexed Hawaii as a territory. Brother Dutton was overjoyed at the news because he was not only a Civil War veteran, but also an avid American patriot. Close to his cottage in Molokai, there was a flagpole where every morning he formally raised and saluted the American flag. It was then taken down at dusk. This pride in his own country he also instilled in his patients, who took

The Church of St. Philomena

the ceremony very seriously, even before the Hawaiian Islands became a United States Possession.

In 1908 Brother Dutton became aware that the Great White Fleet of American ships was sailing around the world. He let it be known that he hoped that the ships might sail past the Settlement, so the residents could see them. His wish eventually came to the attention of President Theodore Roosevelt, who sent a Presidential Order to Admiral Charles Stillman Sperry, the Chief Commander of the fleet. It instructed him to change course in order to sail past Molokai and give a military salute to Brother Dutton and his people.

On the appointed day, the ships arrived in battle formation, and as each one sailed by the Settlement, the colors were dipped in salute. Brother Dutton and his crew dipped their American flag to return the salute. It was an unforgettable historic moment for Brother Dutton and his lepers to receive such an honor from the American government and its President.

Brother Dutton's patriotism was also demonstrated during WWI when he assisted in the war effort by selling war bonds. Even the residents who had little money took up a collection to help the troops. Since Brother Dutton had no money because he had refused any salary, he donated one of his few personal possessions, a pair of binoculars, and sent them to the War Department. He received notification from Franklin D. Roosevelt, the Secretary of the Navy, informing him that his binoculars were actually being used on a battleship. At the end of the war, they were returned, along with a certificate which Brother Dutton framed and kept in his office.[8]

The annexation of Hawaii as a Territory of the United States brought many benefits to the leper colony at Molokai. The United States legislature began to appropriate funds for the maintenance of the Settlement, and the Board of Health made every effort to improve the living conditions of the residents and provide for their needs.

Brother Dutton lowering the American flag

Brother Dutton and the residents saluting the flag

A few ships from The Great White American Fleet

Brother Dutton seated on a stone wall outside his office

Brother Dutton's organizational abilities served him well in managing the expansion of the Settlement. Part of his success was due to his emphasis on making the residents realize that they were not alone. As part of a community, they could help each other and accomplish what they might not be able to do on their own. Some of the men were taught the rudiments of construction. They helped build each other's houses, which gave them a sense of pride. With the skills they learned in doing this, those who were strong enough could then be hired out to work at the Settlement, and receive government payment for their services, enabling them to contribute to the support of their families. Others were encouraged to raise chickens or grow crops. These possibilities showed the residents they could help improve their own lives and this gave them hope. Even the boys were encouraged to help each other and to find opportunities to do some gardening or other small tasks to earn some money. A gym was built for them so they could exercise and build up their strength to remain as healthy as possible. Schools were started for the girls as well as for the boys. The girls' residence, which was named The Bishop Home, was the responsibility of the Franciscan Sisters. It was directed by Mother Marianne Cope, who worked in

Molokai for over thirty years and was later declared a Saint.

One of the things that impressed Brother Dutton when he first arrived in Molokai, was that in this place of such great beauty, where nature blossomed so abundantly, there could also be found so much suffering and pain. Reflecting on this at a later time, he said, "I came to realize that perhaps the beauties of nature can, to a certain extent, relieve physical and mental suffering,"[9] Perhaps this was why when Brother Dutton provided for the construction of buildings, he also made plans to surround them with shade trees, coconut and other fruit trees, bushes and flowering plants in order to add to the beauty of the Colony.

Although Brother Dutton, while in Molokai, lived a life of physical isolation from the world, socially he remained very connected. He kept a running correspondence with the many friends he had made throughout his life. The photograph shown below, which he sent to one of his friends, reveals his sense of humor. Due to the interest created by Father Damien's death, people throughout the world began to focus on the work taking place at Molokai and on Brother Dutton. He

Photo of Brother Dutton signed:
"With compliments of the original"[10]

Maria von Trapp, the Trapp Family Singers and
Father McDonough at the gravesite of Brother Dutton

began to receive hundreds of letters from all over the world asking questions, sending donations, requesting photographs, and even wanting to come and visit the site. Articles about him were also written which praised him and the work he was doing. However, Brother Dutton had no interest in gaining personal popularity. In fact, he responded to this notoriety by saying, "All these writers make me out a hero, while I don't feel a bit like one. I don't claim to have done any great things; I am merely trying in a small way to help my neighbor and my own soul."[11]

Brother Dutton's heroic life ended in 1931. He had devoted forty-five years of service improving and inspiring the lives of those living in the Settlement; and now they mourned and missed him, while the world praised and honored his life of service. Tributes were received from many nations written by ordinary people, as well as by world leaders. President Calvin Coolidge perhaps said it best: "Whenever his story is told, men will pause to worship. His faith, his work, his self-sacrifice appeal to people because there is always something of the same

spirit in them. Therein lies the moral power of the world. He realized a vision that we all have."[12]

In 1949 Blessed Sacrament Church was built in Stowe, Vermont on the site of the farm where Dutton was born, and was declared to be a memorial to his life. Brother Dutton's humanitarian efforts were dramatically illustrated by the artist, André Girard, who created huge murals that decorated the sides of the church which honored his memory.

Three years later, the pastor, Father Francis E. McDonough, Maria von Trapp, and The Trapp Family Singers, made a special journey to Molokai to attend a mass and give a concert as a tribute to Brother Dutton. Upon their arrival, they visited his grave at the Settlement. As was recalled by Maria von Trapp in her book, *A Family on Wheels;* "Gently, Johannes placed our Mount Mansfield pine wreath at the foot of the cross. With Father McDonough leading, each one of us added a lei to the grave . . ."[13] It was a loving and fitting tribute from the people of Stowe, Vermont to their native son.

Brother Dutton at his office reviewing his memoirs

In order to truly understand the sacrifice Brother Dutton made in going to Molokai, one has to consider that as far back as Biblical times, leprosy had been one of the most dreaded diseases, not only because of the progressive deterioration and disfigurement of the body, but because those having the disease were considered to be highly contagious, and had to be isolated from the rest of society. In addition to this, there was no successful treatment or cure. When Joseph Dutton made the decision to go to Molokai, Father Damien had already contracted the disease after serving there only a few years. Dutton had to realize there was a strong possibility that he might eventually face the same fate. It took a man of great courage, dedication and love for humanity to make the decision he did.

During Brother Dutton's tenure at Molokai every effort was made to find treatments suitable to help those afflicted with the illness but none were successful.

Since the times of Brother Dutton and Father Damien many changes have taken place. The term leprosy has been changed to Hansen's Disease, to honor Gerhard Armauer Hansen, the Norwegian physician who discovered the leprosy bacillus. Scientists have also brought about many advancements in controlling the disease. Although the complete elimination of the illness has not been achieved, methods and medications have been developed to control its progress. The World Health Organization has seen to it that patients having Hansen's Disease can now receive free treatment all over the world, and be considered acceptable members of society,[14] except in a few countries such as India, Brazil and some African countries where they have not been able to control the disease.[15]

Some inhabitants of the Molokai Colony left the original Settlement and relocated elsewhere, while others chose to remain in the Molokai area because this was the place where they felt most at home. The peninsula at Kalaopapa in Molokai was declared a National Historic Park in 1980. Everyone can now visit there, and appreciate its natural beauty as well as reflect on its extraordinary history.

TRIBUTES, MEMOIRS AND LETTERS

Brother Dutton has the unique distinction of having received tributes from five Presidents of the United States. In addition to tributes from Presidents Theodore Roosevelt and Calvin Coolidge described earlier in this chapter, on May 20th, 1923 President Warren G. Harding wrote a long personal letter to Brother Dutton stating in part, "You have set for us a model which I wish might be raised up for the view and emulation of many others, for it is in the selfless service of our brothers that all of us must at last find the great satisfactions and consolations of this life."[16]

After Brother Dutton's death Franklin D. Roosevelt, then serving as Governor of New York, stated, "The man of faith perceives in Brother Dutton a providential supplement to Father Damien with whom he labored. These two lives linked together in the heroic and gentle ministrations to the unfortunate lepers on Molokai stand out as beacons, guides to better things, encouragement in distress, and inspirations to sacrifice for their fellow men."[17]

President Herbert Hoover wrote of him, "I am deeply interested in the romantic story of Brother Joseph Dutton, whose life as a pioneer, soldier, and great humanitarian is so characteristic of our people in its variety, picturesqueness and idealism. The service to the lepers of Molokai crowned his life with a saintly glory. . . ."[18]

The most unusual tribute sent to Brother Dutton from The White House was perhaps a package from Mrs. Woodrow Wilson which contained her inaugural bouquet when her husband was made President. Although it arrived in a rather damaged condition, her gesture spoke volumes of her regard for his life of humanitarian service.[19]

Despite the many tributes Brother Dutton received from important personages, the tribute that he probably would have appreciated the most was the one written in a letter by Father Damien to Father Hudson in which he stated, "The courage of my Dear brother Joseph Ira B. Dutton appears to respond very well to the special calling for which our Blessed Lord has chosen him. He takes a special interest in all that concerns the altars and sacristies of our churches-Being now myself on the list of the unclean I leave to his care all what belongs to the Lord's and Priest's houses-and . . . he also acts as our Druggist-and He's truly a good confrere to me."[20]

Probably the most credible tributes an individual can receive are not the ones from people who admire them from afar, but rather from those who have actually witnessed their lives and challenges. Doctor Arthur A. Mouritz, the resident physician of the Colony, who for years observed Brother Dutton as he attended to his daily tasks, wrote the following description of his work at the Settlement, ". . . whatever Brother Dutton undertook to do he did it well. . . . He always seemed to find time to attend to the numerous duties that fell to his lot, the more his work expanded the better he seemed to like it . . . I enumerate some of Brother Dutton's manifold duties performed daily: Father Damien's companion, secretary, servant, nurse and other menial work, sexton, sacristan, verger, purveyor for Father Damien's homes and his household, hospital steward, dresser, clinical clerk, later manager of the Baldwin Home, sanitary engineer, architect, landscape gardener-the site of the Baldwin Home was formerly a pile of rocks. Brother Dutton was also Postmaster for years, single handed and alone, he filled well all of the above offices."[21]

Brother Dutton never formally wrote his memoirs, but fortunately in 1931 a reporter by the name of Howard D. Case was assigned by the *Honolulu Star-Bulletin* to go to Molokai and visit Brother Joseph Dutton in order to obtain his life story. Sadly, within the year, Brother Dutton died. Howard Case subsequently edited a book entitled, *Brother Joseph Dutton His Memoirs*, in which he presented informal conversations with Brother Dutton as he answered questions and recalled and reflected on various times in his life.

The foreword to the book was written by Wallace R. Farrington, former Governor of Hawaii who stated, "Lives that live forever are lives of self-sacrifice. So the deeds of Joseph Dutton will live in the minds of men and be re-told for generations, while those of his day generally classed as successful will be . . . forgotten."[22]

In preparing the memoirs, Howard Case had access to Brother Dutton's papers. The following words found on a scrap of paper among his things, give us a possible glimpse of Brother Dutton's reflections on his own life's journey, "Thus we go on striving and progressing, trying and failing, each one advancing in the ways of God, we hope . . . day by day, under the mighty mountains, verdure-clad, 'midst such wondrous creations while the voices in the waves and in the winds proclaim to us, in Nature's grand oratorio, the power and majesty of God."[23]

André Girard at an exhibition

ANDRÉ GIRARD

MASTER ARTIST OF THE 20TH CENTURY

André Girard, the artist who transformed the modest rustic church of Blessed Sacrament into a remarkable work of art, was not only a gifted painter, but an internationally renowned artist.

Through his revolutionary technique of painting on glass using actual light as a pictorial element, he changed the 36 ordinary windows of the church into extraordinary paintings having a stained glass effect. As the natural light of the sun passed through the painted glass, it caused the colors to radiate and reflect within the dimly lit church, to make it seem to glow.

Girard also transformed the story of Brother Joseph Dutton from a small plaque describing his work with the lepers in Molokai, into twelve large ten-foot outdoor murals. These illustrated Brother Dutton's heroic work in Hawaii, in a way people could visually experience his life there.

Born in Chinon, France, in 1901 at the brink of the 20th Century, André Girard's art reflected the beauty of the arts of the past, but also expressed the innovation, freedom and dynamism that were to characterize the art of the new century. When he was 17 and studying classical art at L'Ecole de Beaux Art in Paris, Girard was given the incredible opportunity to live and work with the most acclaimed liturgical artist of the 20th Century, Georges Rouault. The older artist recognized the talent in the young man, and took an interest in his development as an artist. It is believed that Rouault's focus on religious themes as well as his use of layers of color to produce a glowing effect of light had an influence on Girard's own work. But Girard wanted to go far beyond these effects. He wanted to paint with pure transparent color and light itself.

At the age of 20 Girard first experimented with these ideas. Asked to paint a curtain that would be the background for the reading of a play, Girard broke with tradition and did a series of paintings on glass that could be projected by a lantern slide to provide changes in scenery and mood. The experiment was so successful, Girard did similar projections for various plays, including William Shakespeare's, "Measure for Measure". In 1925 the young Girard started to receive professional recognition by being selected to do a poster for the International Exhibition of Decorative Arts in Paris. Girard's international reputation was further enhanced when in 1937 he was commissioned to do several murals for the International Paris Exhibition. It continued when he was appointed Director of the French Pavilion of the San Francisco World's Fair, for which he did several murals. In 1940 he also executed several murals for the French Pavilion at the New York World's Fair.

During this time the young Girard met a girl named Andrée, who not only became his wife and mother of their four daughters, but a life-long companion and participant in his many artistic achievements.

Unfortunately, World War II interrupted his artistic career, but André Girard developed a way to utilize his artistic talent to help his country. He became a caricaturist that cleverly ridiculed the Gestapo, for the amusement of his compatriots. He also volunteered and became a liaison officer for the French Underground Resistance Movement. As an artist he had a reasonable excuse to travel to different cities to deliver his work. This provided the perfect means for secret messages and plans to be communicated throughout France. Girard's clandestine activities were finally discovered, and he narrowly escaped to England where he provided detailed information about the French Underground to British Intelligence. He was then sent to the United States to share his cumulative knowledge to benefit the Allied Forces. At the end of the war, President Truman awarded him the Legion of Merit, in recognition of his valuable assistance in furthering the war effort. Girard's wife, Andrée, who had been arrested as a courier and sent to various concentration camps in France, received the Legion d'Honneur from the French government for services to her country during the war.

When the war ended, the Girards decided to make their home in the United States. The following pages illustrate Girard's continued growth and development as an artist after WWII.

NYACK AND PARIS RESIDENCES

View from the Girard's residence in Nyack

Although the Girards' first home in America was in Princeton, New Jersey, they eventually settled on a more permanent basis in a large old Victorian house in Nyack, New York. The apartment and studio were located on a hill overlooking the Hudson River Valley. They enjoyed this view so much that André Girard decided to paint it across four large canvas panels that formed a folding screen, so they could continue to enjoy seeing this same view even when they were in Paris.

However, these panels were more than just the view from their windows because Girard personalized these paintings. He included a comfortable couch beneath the windows with a palette, paint, and brushes resting on the right side of the couch and on the left, (missing from the photograph), was his wife, Andrée, leisurely reading a book. The screen was a charming, subtle and innovative way to portray the beautiful view as well as their relationship and home life.

Since André Girard frequently exhibited throughout Europe, the Girards maintained a second residence in Paris, France. The apartment had a huge studio attached and the front windows had wrought iron balconies with a view of the Moulin Rouge, the cabaret made famous by Toulouse Lautrec's artwork. This was a perfect setting for Girard to continue to add to France's artistic heritage.

Like most 20th century artists living in Paris, André Girard maintained an atelier. This was a combination studio-art gallery, where artists could work at their craft and at the same time be prepared to professionally display their work to potential customers.

Until its close in 2016, Girard's atelier was the only one that had continualy been in use to display the work of the original artist. It had been used to store and sell his works as well as to plan for future exhibitions. Occasionally it offered young artists the opportunity to display their artwork in the attached gallery.

The French government has designated this area of the city as a historic art site. The official marker explaining its historic significance was placed directly in front of the Atelier André Girard.

Mrs. Andrée Girard at their apartment in Paris

TRAVELS

André and Andrée Girard travelled frequently. One of the places they most enjoyed visiting was the city of Venice. Their first trip was to last a few days, but André Girard became so charmed by the historic character of the city, the beauty of its exotic architecture, and the pageantry of its culture, that they eventually stayed for three months.

In reminiscing about his visits to Venice, André Girard once recalled how he used to rent a little rowboat and set forth each morning exploring the canals and stopping at various spots to make sketches. Needless to say, he got in the way of the gondoliers who would shout incomprehensible insults to him in Italian, to which Girard would respond with equal enthusiasm in French. The gondoliers eventually realized Girard didn't even understand them and they became more resigned to the futility of arguing with this stubborn Frenchman. Some even became curious about his sketches and asked to see them. These small sketches later became the basis for many of his paintings and prints.

Canal in Venice

Sketch of a street in Jerusalem

The Girards travelled to many places, but their most important journey was to the Holy Land. Artists throughout the ages had painted religious subjects without ever being where these events had taken place. Girard, however, took his Bible with him as he visited each traditional site, so he could see, hear, feel, and be an authentic witness to the atmosphere, culture, and visual characteristics he experienced. In 1961, Girard wrote an article for *The Critic* magazine, entitled "An Artist in the Holy Land", in which he stated: "A silent echo exists in Palestine which is never too tired to speak to the visitor and under many forms, Jesus himself is present on the stage of his love for humanity. It may take time to feel it. It is certainly useful to be guided by the sacred scriptures."[24] Girard indeed was guided and inspired by what he experienced there. The stories from the Bible became one of the most important themes of his work for the rest of his life.

SILK-SCREEN PRINTING

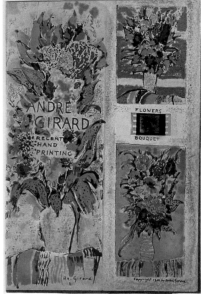

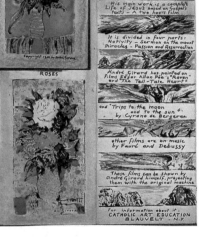

André Girard's Silk-Screened Artist Brochure

*From "Trip to the Other World"
by Cyrano de Bergerac*

Repose is in Change

During the 1950s, Girard experimented with serigraphy, the silk-screen method of printing. At this time artists' hand-screened prints were usually limited to the use of a few basic colors, due to the need to create different screens for the original image as well as each successive color. These screens had to be perfectly matched to create a successful print. Girard, unaware of the limitations of the medium, approached it as a painter with remarkable results. He achieved prints that were so rich in color, texture, detail, shading, and highlights they rivaled the effects of paintings.

Not content to merely produce individual prints, during a period of eight years André Girard created a series of limited edition hand-printed books in English and in French, which can be found in the Rare Books Collections of several museums, libraries, and universities, including Marquette University, Queensborough Community College, and the National Library in Paris. The variety of effects he achieved and the quality of the prints reproduced on these pages, are evidence of Girard's extraordinary creative abilities.

*Portrait of
Mrs. Andrée Girard
reading a book*

Everything has a Beginning and an End

*The one who despairs
will not gain hope because it is by definition
impossible and inaccessible*

25

LITURGICAL ART

Among André Girard's most important artistic achievements were his liturgical works. Starting in 1949, Girard was given the exceptional opportunity to decorate several churches. Among these were: Blessed Sacrament Church in Stowe, Vermont; The Church of Saint Anthony, Napara Park, New York; and St. Ann's Chapel at Stanford University, Palo Alto, California.

Designing completely different decorations for each of the churches was a major artistic challenge, but André Girard succeeded in creating for each church a unique spiritual atmosphere suited to its size, setting, congregation and religious functions.

By studying the cover of the proposal Girard submitted for the decoration of Blessed Sacrament Church, it is possible to see that he had not only understood Brother Dutton's devotion to his congregation in Molokai, but Girard had also been able to express the relationship and meaning Brother Dutton's work had for Blessed Sacrament Church. At this early stage of planning, Girard's simple sketch also captured the likeness, character and personality of this son of Stowe.

André Girard's paintings for St. Ann's Chapel at Stanford University were quite different from those he designed for Blessed Sacrament Church. The four vertical windows of St. Ann's reach the full height of the chapel and bathe it in color and light. Counterbalancing the dramatic effect of the windows were the *Stations of the Cross* on the opposite wall. The paintings are done

Cover of proposal for Blessed Sacrament Church

Sketch of
The Temptation of Christ
and completed window

26

on large-scaled vertical panels that encompass your visual space. Although the figures are not quite life-sized, the paintings are placed on raised platforms so that the figures are seen almost at your own level. You view the face of Christ as He passes before you carrying His cross, then as you approach the next panel, you suddenly have to look down because He has fallen at your feet. This creates an interactive participation between the viewer and what is taking place that is highly effective. This side of the church is darkened and the drama of each scene is enhanced because each Station is lit by natural light that enters through a series of vertical openings strategically placed on the wall. Be assured that following the *Way of the Cross* at St. Ann's Chapel is a compelling experience, not easily forgotten.

Concept submitted for window
of Saint Ann's Chapel

Two sections of the Way of the Cross

FILM INNOVATIONS

In 1961, André Girard's international reputation as an artist whose religious works were highly dramatic and impactful received recognition in Hollywood. The noted producer-director, George C. Stevens of 20th Century Fox Studios, used André Girard as an artistic consultant for the filming of his epic movie, on the life of Christ, *The Greatest Story Ever Told*. Girard spent over three months recreating the atmosphere, streets and buildings of old Jerusalem as well as rendering hundreds of sketches and paintings on the life of Christ to be used as suggestions for the filming of the movie.

Girard's paintings had also been shown on television during religious holidays and been favorably reviewed. However, after viewing his artwork on television, Girard became aware that his paintings looked static in a medium that thrived on visual movement and constantly changing images. He immediately set forth to find a solution to this problem, and with the help of his wife, Andrée, Girard developed the idea of adapting his concept of "painting on light" which he had used on glass windows, to be implemented by means of painting on 70 mm film.

Using inks, glazes, stained-glass paints, and enamels, Girard painted scenes on long strips of film that had an extended visual span so they could be effortlessly transitioned from one scene to the next. As the film was passed through a horizontal filmstrip projector, movement was achieved, and as the images passed across the light the colors became gloriously more vibrant. Since the color white was actually pure light passing through clear film, it added to the intensity of the images.

The final effect was as if one was viewing a continuous mural of stained glass passing before you illustrating the story. The visual impact was further enhanced by variations in the pace of the movement, the addition of sound and music, as well as the accompanying narrative

Working with special enlarging glasses on 70 mm film, Girard paints narrative scenes with infinite detail

Sections of the crucifixion and the resurrection

readings. Girard's films using this innovative technique were particularly suited to television because they blended all these elements to create an astonishing and overwhelming impact on the viewer.

Throughout the years CBS, ABC and NBC featured Girard's hand-painted films on various programs including: *The Sermon on the Mount, The Passion and Resurrection, The Catholic Hour*, and *The Hallmark Christmas Festival*. The films were considered to be so unique and innovative that Girard was presented with the Television Arts Award of the National Council of Catholic Men.

From 1959 to 1968 Girard continued to focus on the production of hand-painted films. They not only varied in the techniques he used, but in the subject matter. Even Girard's use of sounds added greatly to the impact of his imagery. For the film, *The Tell-tale Heart* by Edgar Allen Poe, Girard used actual recordings of the beatings of a human heart at various speeds and intensities to suggest the growing anxiety and tension of each moment. For the short-film entitled *The Bells,* Girard travelled throughout Europe visiting the great cathedrals as well as little churches, recording the pealing of their bells. The combined sounds created a musical symphony of their own. In the film *Homage to Venice and Claude Debussy*, Girard used the composer's Water Pieces to enhance the visual experience of gliding through the waters of its canals.

I first encountered André Girard's films in 1962 through a double-spread article that appeared in a Sunday edition of the *New York Mirror Magazine.** I was drawn by the beauty and power of the paintings and intrigued by the description of the extraordinary technique through which these hand-painted images

Girard showing one of his hand-painted films on his specially built projector

could achieve continuous movement to illustrate narratives of the Bible. The article mentioned André Girard had a studio in Nyack, New York. Although I called several times, each time I was informed the number had been disconnected. Since computers and the internet had not been developed at this time, I eventually put aside my search but kept the article.

Several years later when I began teaching at St. Joseph's College in Brooklyn, New York, fate intervened. During a conversation with the college President, Sr. Vincent Thérèse, I happened to mention my search for André Girard, and I was astonished when she said she knew him, and would be happy to help me connect with him.

André Girard subsequently showed several of his films at the college, and exhibited in our art gallery. He also invited me to join the art class he was teaching at Queensborough Community College in Bayside, New York. I was overjoyed at the unexpected opportunity this presented for me.

---

* The use of the first person singular in this instance and throughout the rest of this book refers to the author Josephine Belloso.

from the hand-painted film, "Passion and Resurrection"

Leaded stained glass window
Christ Preaching on the Sea of Galilee

GIRARD'S STUDIO COURSE

André Girard's studio class was different from the typical art course. The same personal care and guidance Girard had received from his own friendship and association with his teacher, Georges Rouault, he extended to his own students. He expressed such confidence in their potential, that they did their best to fulfill his expectations of them. When the Easter break would have interrupted our classes Girard, invited the class to work at his home and studio.

The first time we visited his home in Nyack was an amazing experience for each of us. It was like being transported back in time to the studio of a great 18th century master artist. In 1982 I described our first visit as follows:

"Girard's entire home was bursting its seams with artistic creations. Not only were there limitless numbers of painted canvases, prints, and drawings, but the

Experimental glass pieces

walls and doors in every room and hallway, the drapes, couch covers, bedspreads and tablecloths, and even steps leading to the upper floor, were covered with Girard's creative efforts. But the culminating experience was viewing three of his incredibly beautiful films."[25] A rather shy young student who rarely spoke was so moved by Girard's films, he spoke non-stop about them for the two-hour return ride home.

One of the works which attracted our attention during that first visit was a large leaded stained-glass panel with the theme of Christ preaching on the shores of the Sea of Galilee. The sun was placed directly behind the head of Jesus creating the effects of a halo with light radiating out from there. Since we spent the entire day at Girard's home we witnessed the changes that took place on the scene from the early morning light to the golden tones of sunset and finally the dimming light of dusk. It was a complete and captivating visual transformation.

Placed near this piece were several smaller, experimental panels on which Girard had used enamels and small chunks of glass fired in a kiln to create color and textural effects. These free-form experiments became the basis for a huge, stained-glass image of an angel for a mausoleum he took us to visit. Unfortunately, I did not have my camera with me but the glowing ethereal image of that angel floating in space as the sun bathed it in radiant light is forever engraved in my mind.

André Girard was a caring, encouraging and inspiring teacher. He not only took an interest in his students' artwork, but also in their personal lives. I remember when my father became seriously ill and was facing a

André Girard working in his studio

critical operation, I expressed my concern to Girard about my fear of losing him. To my great surprise several days later, I received a beautiful hand-written note from him personally encouraging me to pray and put my trust in God. The most moving part of the letter was the closing, in which he wrote he hoped I would accept him as my father in art because it would afford him great satisfaction to give me guidance and counsel. It was such a thoughtful and caring thing for him to do.

Our art class continued to meet over the summer at the college studio as well as the Girard home because for André Girard, art did not take a vacation; it was part of one's everyday existence. Sadly, on September 2, 1968, just as the new fall term was about to begin, André Girard passed away from a heart attack at the age of 67. It was devastating news to all who had admired and appreciated him as a remarkable artist, teacher and friend. The newspaper media recorded his passing and the CBS network presented an hour-long feature commemorating his life and work.

Soon after his passing Mrs. Girard asked me to restore some of his films. She explained that each time the original films were shown, the heat from the projector melted some of the paint which then stuck to the reverse side of the films as they were re-wound. It was important to restore them now, so they could be copied onto 35mm film. The prospect of repairing Girard's films was a little frightening. However, due to André

Girard's excellent tutelage and more than a few fervent prayers, I managed to restore the five films on the life of Christ, as well as his latest film, *The Story of Abraham*.

During the final period of André Girard's professional life he had reached an artistic peak. He had not only received international acclaim for his many artistic accomplishments, but he had just completed perhaps one of his most important films, *The Story of Abraham*. Originally commissioned by the State of Israel, the hand-painted film was first shown at one of the events celebrating the inauguration of Dr. Kurt R. Schmeller as the President of Queensborough Community College. In attendance at the premier showing were the U.N. Ambassador from France and the U.N. Ambassador from the State of Israel.

A section of the film of *The Story of Abraham* also served as an inspiration for the noted composer, Richard Yardumian. Maryville College in Tennessee had commissioned him to compose an original musical piece to celebrate the 150th anniversary of the college. The Oratorio which Yardumian composed to accompany the film was presented, through the combined talents of five vocal soloists, a double mixed chorus, and a full orchestra. It was also presented in the city of Philadelphia as well as in England in the prestigious Royal Albert Hall of London.

A year after his death, five of André Girard's films were presented at New York City's Alice Tully Hall at Lincoln Center and plans for commemorative exhibitions of his work were made in the United States as well as in Paris, France.

Concert Cover from The Story of Abraham

Detail of the Adoration Altarpiece

André Girard was a gifted multi-faceted artist. His creative imagination and innovative spirit, his versatility as an artist, as well as the sheer number of important works produced during his lifetime, are truly impressive.

Color and light were the underlying principles that characterized his work; whether it was the changing light of day illuminating the colors of his paintings on glass, the shimmering light reflections on the water in his painting of a Venetian canal, the use of radiant light suggesting a Divine Presence or even the soft glowing light emmanating from the painting of a Madonna and Child, symbolizing their love.

Light effectively created a mood, intensified a dramatic moment, drew attention to a significant feature, or penetrated the darkness to reveal a hidden secret, or possibly offer a glimmer of hope.

However, the most important light of all, was the spark within him that animated his imagination and illuminated his spirit, giving him his unique artistic vision.

A
TRIBUTE
TO
ANDRÉ GIRARD

The following poem was written as a tribute to André Girard in the year that he died. It effectively captures the spirit of this "painter of light" and the significance of his life and work.

"In My Father's House are Many Mansions—"

—I think there is a mansion there
    With walls and domes of living light,
Which need a kind of painter rare
    To paint God's thoughts and love and might—
And here on earth one did prepare
    Himself for such a task aright.

On film against a light opaque
    He drew the passion of the Lord,
Painting with vibrant hues to make
    A "new-expression" of the Word.
A chime of colors which could wake
    Mankind as with a mighty chord.

He drew his own life on the night
    Of worlds at war and bitter crime;
But God! he painted it with light
    Upon the darkness of his time
He flung his spirit at the blight
    And made the raving colors chime.

He taught the young with word and deed:
(A man can teach but what he *is*!)
To help with generous God-speed;
    And such a kindly love was his
As in the legends old we read
    The saints bestowed on those in need.

AURELIA GRETHER SCOTT, PhD[26]
Professor Emeritus
Queenborough Community College

RESTORATION OF A HERITAGE

A PERSONAL CHALLENGE
JUNE – JULY – AUGUST 1974 – 1975

My first visit to Blessed Sacrament Church was like making a journey to a sacred place. After André Girard had passed away, the students he had taught at Queensborough Community College wanted to commemorate what he had meant to them, and thus connect with him again. A few of us decided the most meaningful way to accomplish this would be to make a group pilgrimage to Stowe, and visit the church he had once described to us with such feeling. Girard had painted several churches during his lifetime but the Blessed Sacrament Church in Stowe was the first, and he seemed to have a special remembrance of it.

We left early one morning from New York on our journey to Stowe. Upon arriving we walked around the church and viewed the twelve large-scale murals depicting the lives of Brother Dutton and Father Damien. Painted with bold strokes in black against the raw wood, the murals are powerful in their impact as they sensitively present a continuing narrative of life in the leper colony. It is amazing how Girard was able to create scenes of such beauty while encompassing the harsh reality of everyday life in this isolated place on Molokai.

When I entered the church I was first captivated by how the sunlight pierced through the colors of the windows, creating a beautiful tapestry to illuminate the darkness within; and then, viewing each window more closely, I was also very moved by the expressive quality of how Girard interpreted each Biblical story. The longer I was there, the more I began to experience and appreciate the deep spiritual and meditative aspect of his vision, and that spoke to me even more. We weren't able to spend enough time there because we had to return to New York the same day, but André Girard

The Blessed Mother as a Child

The Resurection

The Mocking of Jesus

had touched and inspired each of us once more in his own special way.

Our visit to Stowe had been a wonderful experience, but when I returned home I became concerned about the deteriorated condition of André Girard's work. At first glance the windows and murals of Blessed Sacrament Church were still very visually impactful, due to Girard's strong sense of design and the beauty of his colors. However upon closer study, I could see that time and weather had taken their toll. Exterior painting on wood as well as interior painting on glass, when exposed to Vermont's extremes in temperature, did not ensure their permanence. The more I thought about it, the more I realized that the future survival of Girard's work might soon be very much in doubt. I also wondered if anything could be done or would be done to preserve it.

In 1974 Blessed Sacrament Church realized that André Girard's paintings would eventually be lost unless something was done to restore them. Mrs. André Girard was consulted about the problem and she suggested I do the restoration, because I had worked so closely with him and successfully restored his paintings on film. The Pastor, Father Francis L. Flaherty, invited me to visit Stowe, to demonstrate my ability to restore Girard's paintings in a manner that would blend in with his unique style and extraordinary techniques. I was, of

course, very excited to have this unexpected opportunity, and planned the visit during my Easter vacation when I was free from my teaching responsibilities. Father Flaherty was very welcoming. He took me for a tour of the church to view the current condition of the murals and windows. He then suggested I get some rest so I could begin restoring one of the windows early the next morning.

Aside from my anxiety about the actual painting, while working the next morning I realized the church would be in continuous use during my preliminary attempts at restoration. Visitors could be a constant distraction, asking questions and it worried me, given the limited time frame I had for this visit.

My expectations were fulfilled. Every day visitors would come with endless streams of questions about the history of the church, so I appealed to Father Flaherty and he provided me with the necessary literature, so I could give tours of the church while I did the restoration.

Finally, on the very last day in the late afternoon when I was feverishly hurrying to put the finishing touches on one of the windows, I heard someone enter the church. Since I had to leave the next day I promised myself I would try not to waste any more precious moments answering visitors' questions.

Brother Dutton meets the Lepers

Father Damien Hears Confessions

Brother Dutton Assissts at Mass

The Windows: Painting on Light

Restoring the windows often included not only the challenge of blending
my painting with André Girard's, but also dusting
the window sills and cleaning off spider webs

Detail showing section of
deteriorated window

The visitor remained so quiet I completely forgot anyone was there. All of a sudden I heard footsteps coming towards my ladder, then someone clearing their throat, saying "Ahem, Ahem!" I turned to find none other than Maria von Trapp dressed in her Bavarian regalia looking up at me. I was absolutely stunned; this was totally unexpected. Mrs. von Trapp was very gracious, complimenting me on the progress I had made, and she said she was very happy the church was planning to restore Girard's artwork. At the end of our conversation she said "I would like to shake your hand, but you are up too high . . ." I immediately thought, oh my goodness, this is the Baroness! Needless to say, I hurried down the ladder and stretched out my hand, only to find it was covered with red, blue, green, yellow and black paint. As I sheepishly withdrew my hand, she said with an amused expression, "When you come back to Stowe, you must come to visit me so I can really shake your hand."

Father Flaherty was very pleased with the window I had restored, and said he looked forward to my return. I was absolutely thrilled to learn I would have the opportunity of preserving André Girard's magnificent windows. My exhilaration diminished considerably when Father Flaherty continued, explaining the restoration would include not only the 36 windows, but also the twelve 10-foot murals, the huge pediment and the doors. It was all a bit overwhelming, but how could I not do all that was within my power to preserve André Girard's artistic and spiritual heritage?

I explained to Father Flaherty, since I was teaching full-time at St. Joseph's College, I only had three months free in the summers and two weeks at Easter. He replied that I could be given a total of six-and-a-half months within the next two years to complete the entire restoration. I took a deep breath and agreed to do it.

*Unrestored Transfiguration
viewed from outdoors*

*Restored window
of the Transfigration
viewed from indoors*

When I returned to Stowe that June, I set forth with great enthusiasm to meet all challenges. Reality set in when I ran out of rags the very first week. Father Flaherty came to my rescue by setting up a collection box at the back of the church, with a sign which read: Clean cotton rags for Josephine. The parishioners responded most generously to the appeal, and I was most grateful.

Although I had already restored André Girard's paintings on film, restoring his work on the windows proved to be quite different. In painting the windows Girard had used oil paints mixed with spar varnish, and applied the paint in layers. Opaque areas of paint were juxtaposed against transparent and translucent areas to achieve a dramatic effect as the light passed through the colors. The result was that the painted effect created on each side of the glass was quite a bit different and yet

had to make visual sense. The lower halves of most of the windows had been greatly affected by extremes in temperature and were flaking, so when the new paint was applied, the old colors sometimes started to peel away even more. Some areas were completely missing. It was not going to be easy . . .

My ultimate goal was not only to fill in the missing areas, but to match the colors perfectly, and blend my brushstrokes so well into Girard's that they would be completely integrated and fused with his original painting, preserving its integrity. In the above photographs one can see two views of The Transfiguration. One photograph shows the window before the restoration, viewed from the outside; the other shows the same scene after the restoration, seen from the interior of the church with the fullness of its glory renewed.

THE EXTERIOR MURALS

Murals on the western side of the church

Since I wasn't quite sure how I was going to solve the problems presented by restoring the exterior murals, I decided to try working them out at the same time as I worked on the windows. Blessed Sacrament Church had been constructed of untreated wood panels, so over the years the snow and ice caused the upper surfaces of the wood to wear away. In addition to this, since the wood had not been kiln dried, it still had sap within it. The hot summer sunlight, through the years, drew the sap to the surface, where it blistered when it mixed with the varnish. Each panel had several of these sticky sections, so the restoration involved more than my attempting to recreate André Girard's bold and beautiful paintings. It also meant that an endless amount of sanding had to be done to remove the blistered surfaces and draw out the remaining sap. I used an electric sander for the larger spaces but the more detailed areas required sanding by hand.

Fortunately, two of my graduating seniors from St. Joseph's College had gotten curious about the project I was doing in Stowe and decided to visit me. I welcomed them with open arms and immediately put them to work sanding. One of the students decided to stay for several weeks and proved to be a great help in driving to the local art stores to refurbish my diminishing supplies. In fact, providentially she became the link

that resulted in my being involved in the 2010–2013 restoration.

Every week groups as well as individuals came to visit Blessed Sacrament Church. Nuns often visited on their vacations. I would always try to ask them what Order they were from because André Girard had painted a mural illustrating the arrival of the Franciscan Sisters who had come to help Brother Dutton in caring for the lepers. I was a little disappointed about not meeting any Franciscan Sisters the first year, but a group of three finally arrived the second year. I explained the story to them, and they were so touched and proud that they asked me to take a photograph of them standing by the mural. I was happy to oblige.

On one occasion, a tour guide swept quickly through the church, and with a monotonous memorized patter, he described each feature of the church. He preceded each statement by pointing and saying "And here we have . . ." I was on a ladder at the very back of the church when he came by. He was completely surprised to discover me, but recovered quickly and paused only for a moment before dramatically exclaiming "And here we have . . . Michelangelo!" Everyone laughed, and so did I, but I have to admit, I was secretly pleased by his reference, even if uttered in jest.

An example of the many areas of the murals where the sap had been drawn to the surface and then blistered

The endless process of sanding

The Franciscan Sisters — past and present

The Annunciation — unrestored above and restored below

I tried to take photographs of the windows as I progressed, but the Pastor said I shouldn't waste my time doing that. I therefore started taking photographs during his dinner hour, but he found out about it and started coming by after dinner and would make pleasant conversation followed by the inevitable question "When do you think you can finish?" This eventually progressed to "Do you think you will ever finish on time?" I am glad I followed my own inclinations to take photographs, because those few clandestine photographs played a significant role in the 2010–2013 restoration.

I'm particularly pleased I got a very clear photograph of the window depicting *The Agony In The Garden.* It is one of Girard's most striking and inspiring pieces. In the photo of *The Annunciation* window, it

The Agony in the Garden—Above: exterior view unrestored
Below: interior view after restoration

is quite noticeable that a major part of the image had flaked off. In fact, the glass was so bare that some of the green colors seen through the angel's wings and robe were actually real trees outside the church. By studying the small flakes of color left on the glass I was able to recreate and seamlessly blend the translucent colors of the angel's garment. This particular painting was located in an inaccessible part of the church; I had to restore it

sitting cross-legged on top of a huge boiler that was in the church at that time.

During this time, my sister, Elly, came to visit me and brought along my nine-year old nephew, Billy, who sang in a boys' choir. He had been looking forward to the visit because *The Sound of Music* was his favorite movie, and he had learned Maria von Trapp lived in Stowe. He was enthusiastically anticipating meeting her.

Maria von Trapp, my nephew Billy,
and Maria's daughter Mitzi von Trapp

Painting above the boiler
with my assistant

Considering his youthful impulsive nature, I warned him Mrs. von Trapp did not like people suddenly interrupting her, and that Father Flaherty had told me she disliked being photographed.

After a few days of listening to him beg for an introduction, I gave in and invited Maria von Trapp and one of her daughters to tea. I was happily surprised they accepted, and with the help of my sister, prepared for the big day. My nephew was on his very best behavior, and actually made a little bow when he was introduced. Mrs. von Trapp was most encouraging and charming, asking him questions about the choir and requesting he sing for her. All of a sudden, Billy disappeared into the bedroom and came out with his little Kodak camera, and asked Mrs. von Trapp if he could take her picture. I held my breath . . . Mrs. von Trapp was very gracious and said "Only if you will pose with me." I breathed a sigh of relief, and took the picture. It came out a little blurry, but it was something my nephew treasured throughout his life.

Father Flaherty had told me he was very concerned and doubtful about the possibility of my being able to restore the plywood doors of the church, because they had become so badly deteriorated. When I inspected them I realized the first layer of plywood had completely disappeared, and the second layer was peeling as well. In addition to this, because the top edges of the plywood had not been protected, water, snow, and ice had penetrated the plywood layers causing them to split. The one saving grace was the painted sections had protected the wood underneath them creating a raised, or relief effect of the images.

Despite the obstacles I decided to try to meet Father Flaherty's challenge. After much research and thoughtful deliberation, I developed a four-step plan. I would use a water-resistant spackle, usually employed in repairing boats, to seal the wood and fill in the cracks. In order to cover the repair work and recreate the appearance of the wood, I would apply a base-coat of tan paint on the doors. After it dried I would use a transparent glaze of brown paint mixed with varnish to create the illusion of wood-graining. Finally, following the raised areas where the paint had protected the wood, I would recreate Girard's original artwork.

I had feared there was no way to salvage the existing doors because they had not only deteriorated on the outer layers but also internally. However, since the Pastor was reluctant to get involved in ordering new doors, at least this restoration recreated the effect Girard initially painted.

While I was doing this process I became curious because several well-dressed gentlemen had started visiting the church during the lunch hour, and asking me technical questions about what I was doing. At first I attributed their visits to religious devotion, but after I had completed the restoration of the doors, one of them confessed that Father Flaherty had sent several parishioners in the field of construction to spy on me because he couldn't figure out what I was doing!

Sequence of the restoration process:
   a—spackle,
   b—base paint,
   c—transparent brown glaze,
   d—black paint to recreate original design

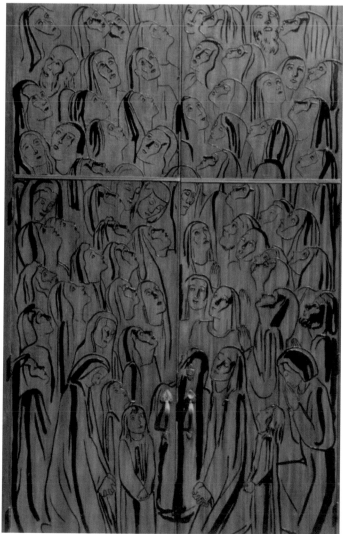

Applying the glaze to simulate the wood grain

The completely restored doors

THE PEDIMENT

My mother had been content receiving my weekly reports by telephone, but when she heard I would have to paint the pediment from a 12-foot high scaffold, she decided it was time for her to visit. The scaffold the workmen constructed for me was free-standing and swayed back-and-forth with my slightest movement. They explained that the scaffold wasn't attached to anything, so it had to be flexible because if it was rigid, it would tip over when I moved. "Don't worry," they said. "You'll get used to the movement and learn to sway with it." At this point, I realized it was futile for me to try to explain to them that I had always had a fear of heights.

The scaffold swayed so much I actually clung to the ladder with both hands as I ascended, leaving my supplies behind. My mother's well-timed arrival proved to be quite helpful. Together we found a solution to get my paints and varnish to the top of the scaffold: we set up a pulley system using a box to hold the supplies. This meant a second sign was added to the back of the church asking for small-to-medium boxes for Josephine. Unfortunately, the only box that proved to be workable came from a case of bourbon, and was so labeled in large print. I can just imagine what this might have suggested to any visitors who observed my mother diligently sending me up a box labeled bourbon each day as I worked.

The restoration of the pediment presented me with the greatest challenge. Upon close examination of the

mural, I was shocked I could only decipher faint traces of unconnected lines. Through the years the original painting had faded so much that workmen who had been hired to paint the trim of the church had mistakenly painted over the mural with redwood stain, covering the entire pediment. In order to be able to accurately recreate André Girard's original painting, I decided to begin by enlarging several early black-and-white photographs of the church. Although the details became blurred with the enlargements, I was at least able to envision the placement of the figures. With this as a basis, I made a more precise drawing which I then followed in recreating the mural.

André Girard did not make it easy. He had painted the pediment as far as the corners on both sides. Since the scaffold did not extend that far, it meant I had to use a three-foot extension on my brush and lie flat on my stomach on that swaying scaffold, in order to reach those elusive corners. I cannot even begin to describe the effect this experience had on my nerves. I still have a fear of heights.

As I began working on the upper sections of the pediment I realized I would need a higher scaffold. However, the workmen refused to add any more height to the existing scaffold because there would not be anything to attach it to. They explained it would be extremely dangerous for me. My difficulty was, the three-foot extension I had been using on my brush could only reach a certain height, and the peak of the pediment had a dramatic image of the Holy Spirit as a dove that had to be restored. After considering my limited options I said a little prayer, attached a five-foot extension to my brush, and delivered the final strokes that completed the restoration of the pediment. It was truly a fulfilling moment for me.

As my time in Stowe was ending I became even more aware of the impact of Girard's artistry. An extraordinary incident occurred as I was finishing the work on the pediment that clearly reaffirmed this for me. A month before I left Stowe, Father Flaherty invited me to a very special dinner at the nearby Trapp Family Lodge to thank me for all the work I had done. When the day finally arrived, Father Flaherty came by to warn me I had to stop working early that afternoon in order to be ready in time for the dinner, because, he said, "Maria von Trapp is not to be kept waiting."

The day of the dinner, I had every intention of heeding Father Flaherty's warning, when I suddenly heard a loud sound of screeching brakes. Fearing an accident I turned to find a tall young man jumping from a huge tractor trailer, coming toward me asking, "What are you doing up there?" Realizing this encounter might cause a delay, I kept my explanations as brief as possible, hoping he would go away. He kept asking questions, so I sent him to look at the murals surrounding the church. He returned, wanting more information, this time about the windows, which were different from any he had ever seen.

In an attempt to distract him further, I suggested he go into the church in order to see the windows with the effect of the late-afternoon sunlight shining through the images. "Oh no," he said. "I haven't been in a church since I was a kid, and I'm not going in now." Realizng his resistance, I suggested he just poke his head in. I was amused to see curiosity eventually got the better of him. He opened the door and leaned in. After a bit of time he was in up to his shoulders, and finally he was down to one foot anchored outside, which eventually disappeared into the church. At that time, Blessed Sacrament Church didn't have a vestibule, and you entered directly into the church proper. At this point, I was planning my escape, when he excitedly emerged from the church, wanting me to tell him all about Girard and the beautiful paintings he had done from the stories in the Bible.

I was very touched by how much he had responded to Girard's work, but I had to get back to the hotel, so I said, "Why don't you come back tomorrow when I'll have plenty of time to tell you all about Girard and the church." I was surprised as he suddenly held me by my shoulders, and said "Look, you don't understand, I'm driving across the country and probably will never come through here again. I need to know more about this man and his paintings. If there were more places like this, I would want to come back to church and to pray." I reluctantly explained that I had to get back to my hotel as soon as possible to get ready for a special dinner. He then enthusiastically suggested I could continue telling him about Girard and this church as he drove me back to the hotel. All the warnings relating to the dangers of getting into a car with a stranger echoed through my mind, but this young man had been so spiritually moved by his visit to this church that I made a mental sign of the cross and climbed into the truck with him. When we got to the hotel, he sincerely thanked me for sharing the story of Girard and this church, and said he hoped that someday he might return again.

I finally got to the special dinner on time, and Father Flaherty presented me with a beautiful hand-blown crystal vase which I was invited to fill with flowers from

This photo shows the hand and sleeve of Father Damien that I started to restore. The rest of his figure and those of two lepers on the right are completely faded.

The scaffold was split in half in order to have access to the extremities of the pediment

Maria von Trapp's private garden. This truly proved to be a memorable day for me for so many reasons.

As the deadline date approached for the restoration to be completed, it began to rain and continued to do so for over 10 days. This created a critical situation because two coats of varnish needed to be applied over the pediment and doors in order to provide the necessary protection for the recently complete artwork. The parishioners had been asked to pray for the rain to stop, but I became so desperate I started asking visitors to pray as well. A lady from a nearby Protestant congregation came by one day and said she would ask her church prayer group to try to help. Within three days, the rain stopped. I waited a couple of days for the surfaces to dry out, and was applying the second layer of varnish to the pediment when the same lovely lady came back to visit. With a wry little smile, she said to me "See? You needed the prayers of the Protestants to get God to listen!" I immediately climbed down from the scaffold, and gave her a hug.

The climax of all my restoration experiences at Stowe occurred when Mrs. Andrée Girard came to view the completed work, and to drive me home. When she arrived, she immediately wanted me to show her each section in detail. I first took her to view the 12 murals of the exterior walls, and then to see the work on the pediment and doors. We then entered the church and viewed the 36 windows. This took close to an hour, and Mrs. Girard had not said one word. I finally suggested she was probably tired from her drive to Stowe, and might like to sit down. She remained silent for a few more minutes, and then turned to me and said "I feel as if André had just finished painting it." My joy was complete.

That evening Father Flaherty and a few parishioners visited the church to say good-bye. I was very moved that Maria von Trapp gave me a hug, and blessed my forehead with the sign of the cross—the same way my Mother blessed me when I was a child.

I still don't know how I ever restored the paintings of 36 windows, 12 murals, a pediment and two doors in six-and-a-half months, except by the grace of God. When I left the next morning I had the satisfaction of knowing all the paintings of Blessed Sacrament Church had been restored. Although I knew the restoration could not last forever, for one brief shining moment André Girard's legacy was luminous and complete once more.

Collage of murals

MURAL RESTORATION SUMMERS 2010–2014

Matthew H. Strong restoring one of the murals

In 2010, Blessed Sacrament Church needed to restore the twelve exterior murals which André Girard had painted, telling the story of Brother Dutton in Molokai. Due to the passage of time, exposure to the elements, and extremes in weather conditions, not only the paint needed to be restored, but the wood base for the murals required restoration as well.

Fortunately, Matthew H. Strong, a local artist, was selected for the commission. Matthew was well-qualified to meet the challenges of the work. He was a recognized artist and master carver, and therefore would be able to develop the best approach to restoring the paintings as well as the deteriorating wood on which they were done. Matthew Strong's first approach to the restoration was to sand around the painted areas, in order to try to preserve the original artwork by André Girard. However, after being informed that the murals had been completely stripped down to the wood by the second restorer in 1994, he decided to sand the panels down completely as well. In this way, he was able to remove the top layers of the deteriorated wood to the more solid pine underneath.

The surprising result was that when the paint was removed, the wood behind the paint was lighter than the darker weathered wood around it. Over the years, the paint had protected the wood underneath it. The value of this lighter image left on the wood was that it created a negative of the original mural that could provide a basic pattern for the restoration. I had also given Matthew photographs of the murals so these could also provide the necessary details that might have faded over the years of the murals' existence.

The final system that Matthew devised for the restoration he described as follows; "My first step was to sand each panel down to clean wood. I then applied clear exterior polyurethane and lightly sanded again. Patterns were then drawn following the negative images and the photographs, after which Black Sign Painter's Paint was used to re-create the original artwork. After several layers of polyurethane and urethane were applied and sanded, the restoration was completed."

This may seem easy to accomplish. However, one has only to compare the murals before and after the restoration to understand the skill, experience and attention to detail that was required to achieve such a successful result. Before the restoration, the murals were rather dark due to the deteriorated state of the wooden panels. By stripping down the wood to the more solid and lighter layers underneath, Matthew achieved a greater contrast to the black painted images, thus making the

Matt seeks to reproduce the original images

murals more impactful. The crisp lines of the recent restoration and re-discovered details also added much to the successful re-creation of the originals.

During the restoration of the murals, Matthew had a young helper. His daughter, Isabelle, donated her time and efforts the first year, and was so diligent and accurate in her work, that Blessed Sacrament hired her the second year. She was allowed to work on one of the murals following her father's drawings. Isabelle became so inspired by the selfless lives of Brother Dutton and Father Damien, that she used the money she earned to go to Central America with her high school the next summer to help the poor and disadvantaged.

André Girard's idea of painting the exterior of Blessed Sacrament Church with murals illustrating the life of Brother Dutton was a bold and inspiring concept. However, since the church was to be dedicated to the Stowe native, the murals seemed the perfect way to make visitors aware of Brother Dutton and the valuable contribution he had made in going to Molokai to help Father Damien in his mission of mercy. Without these extraordinary murals Brother Dutton's accomplishments would probably have been limited to a few words on a plaque which most visitors might overlook. Girard's murals are large and dramatic and draw one's immediate attention and interest.

The scenes Girard painted of Brother Dutton's life in Molokai are devoid of distracting color. Boldly painted in black against the raw wood, they are suited for the rustic tropical setting. The rich, lush vegetation of large leaves and overgrown vines also add a sense of beauty to each scene, despite the serious nature of the subject matter being represented.

André Girard cleverly draws us into each scene by providing a particular vantage point from which we view each event. In most instances, we view the scenes at a distance from behind tropical foliage. In other instances, we view the event inside an architectural setting; or we are brought closer to the scene as if we were standing directly behind the lepers. By changing our vantage point we literally become engaged in the viewing process as we follow in the lives of Brother Dutton, Father Damien and their congregation.

André Girard's narrative of Brother Dutton's life in Molokai is: dramatic in its presentation, expressive in its bold, primitive style; impactful and moving in its effect on the viewer; authentic and true to reality in the portrayal of the challenges Brother Dutton, Father Damien and their flock were facing. The result: once the murals have been experienced, and one has followed in the footsteps of Brother Dutton, the events become enduring images in our memory.

André Girard selected most of the scenes he would illustrate in the murals based on accounts described in *Damien the Leper* by John Farrow, published by Sheed and Ward in 1937. The quotes are under each panel.

Mural before restoration

Mural after restoration

A—The Arrival of Brother Dutton in Molokai

He, Father Damien, was at his usual post of observation, a cluster of rocks on the beach, on the morning that saw the arrival of Dutton . . . The boat grated on the sand and the American stepped ashore to meet the priest. While the latter surveyed him curiously, Dutton briefly explained his ambition and position and stated that he wished no remuneration . . . He had credentials, letters of consent and approval from Bishop Koeckmann and the Board of Health . . . p. 179.[27]

In this first mural, André Girard artistically engages us in following Brother Dutton as he begins his new life of service in Molokai. By enclosing the scene of his arrival with tropical vegetation, Girard creates the illusion we are witnessing the event by peering through an opening in the the foliage.

In this momentous encounter, Brother Dutton is portrayed as vigorously striding forward with eagerness to meet Father Damien, who is shown in a more reserved pose. By positioning both men as they clasp hands, Girard symbolizes their newly-formed alliance.

Upon closer inspection, we can observe greater details that enrich the experience of the event. Huge mountains are visible in the background as well as the sea surrounding the island. Girard also suggests what this moment might have signified for Brother Dutton by portraying the ship that brought him to Molokai as it sails away in the distance, leaving him to face new and unknown challenges.

B—Father Damien Introduces Brother Dutton to the Lepers

As Dutton calmly and unflinchingly gazed upon each successive horror, the priest instinctively seemed to know, without any superfluity of words, that at last here was someone who would understand him, who would work with him in harmony and accord. In the twilight of a fast ebbing life, Damien was to learn that he had found the most precious of human gifts; the jewel of friendship . . . p. 180[28]

André Girard portrays this dramatic scene with little emotional reaction on the part of Brother Dutton as he views the lepers for the first time. The most expressive figures of the scene are the lepers whom Girard portrays eagerly leaning forward as they try to decide if Brother Dutton truly has come to help them. Father Damien initially must have been uneasy about the response of Brother Dutton and whether his resolve would weaken when he realistically confronted the challenges he was facing. The relieved expression on Father Damien's face demonstrates his realization that here at last was a kindred spirit willing to assist him in caring for his flock.

By placing the figures within a structural setting, André Girard gives the viewer the impression that they are within the enclosure as the scene is taking place. The tropical setting is established by having large openings on the walls revealing the sunlight as well as tropical foliage outdoors.

C—Father Damien and Brother Dutton at Work among the Lepers

Damien, as his death approached, was to engage himself in a fever of activity that became almost frantic. With the inroads of disease giving him the same weaknesses as extreme age, he, many times because of failing memory, would leave unfinished a task to commence a new one; and the unfinished task would be sure to be completed by the faithful and tactful Dutton who, following behind, would carefully attack all problems with a methodical carefulness born of his army training; a schooling he never forgot . . . p. 180.[29]

André Girard in this mural illustrates one of the many tasks Br. Dutton had to fulfill since Father Damien's health was beginning to fail. The cleansing and changing of the wrappings for the lepers' wounds had to be accomplished on a regular basis as well as the completion of the many unfinished projects begun by Father Damien.

When Matthew was restoring this mural, he found it puzzling that Father Damien was missing from the scene even though the above quote from the book specifically mentioned him. By referring to an earlier photograph of the mural, Matthew was able to re-create the original mural as Girard had painted it. We can now clearly decipher Father Damien standing behind Br. Dutton ready to provide assistance. A missing woman and a man were also re-created. Restoring these missing figures was an important accomplishment in preserving the integrity of Girard's work. Matthew was amused by this situation and liked to refer to this mural as illustrating, "The years that Father Damien and some of the lepers were lost in the jungle."

Section of mural where Father Damien was missing

D—Brother Dutton Assisting Father Damien at Mass

Dutton was to take care of the two churches and to assist, although he doubted his worthiness, the priest at Mass. As the latter's hands were rapidly becoming too swollen to be of such use, it was also agreed that the newcomer would gradually assume the unpleasant duty of dressing and washing the sores of the lepers at the hospital . . . p. 181[30]

E—The Distribution of Holy Communion

F—Father Damien in the Confessional

A major focus of Father Damien and Brother Dutton was to provide for the spiritual needs of their leper congregation. André Girard on the opposite page creates a scene of Mass being conducted in the great outdoors by Father Damien assisted by Brother Dutton. The lepers are depicted kneeling on the ground in poses that suggest fervent attitudes as they pray and receive the Blessed Sacrament.

Another way in which Father Damien provided religious services was by hearing confessions. The section of the wall on which this mural was painted had an opening for the door of the church sacristy. This presented an arstic challenge, but André Girard cleverly solved the problem by making the door into a confessional, with Father Damien inside and Brother Dutton kneeling to make his confession as several lepers await their turns. The amusing aspect when I was doing the original mural restoration, was to see the figure of Father Damien suddenly swing out from the wall as the priest appeared to hop out behind him when he exited the church after Mass.

The scene also seemed to captivate visitors' attention, and sometimes children posed for photos going to confession with Father Damien. The door was sealed shut when the church building was renovated but it is still possible to discover the outline of the door as well as its hinges.

G—The Burial of the Dead

I (Damien) have also buried a large number. The average of deaths is at least one a day. Many are so destitute that there is nothing to defray their burial expenses. They are simply wrapped in a blanket. As far as my duties allow me time, I make coffins myself for these poor people . . . p. 119.[31]

H—Anguished Lepers Witness the Loss of Supplies

Bad weather would occasionally cause a capsize and, of course, the loss of provisions. Many a time there was enacted the tragedy of starving lepers standing on the sea-beaten beach and watching with anguished eyes while their only hopes for food were engulfed by the angry waves. These were the conditions when the priest came to Molokai. He rapidly caused a change . . . p. 120.[32]

I—Brother Dutton Takes Over Additional Responsibilities

"There is so much left to do." A horizon of achievement continued to beckon him. A new chapel was planned and at the hospital a new building was commenced. In vain Dutton begged him to desist, to rest. His only answer was, "Off I am, Brother Joseph!" and although his pace was sometimes but a stagger off he would go . . . p. 186 [33]

In addition to attending to the spiritual needs of their community, Brother Dutton and Father Damien also had to attend to their physical needs. Food, lodging, and medical attention had to be provided on a daily basis. At the end of their life's journey, provision for their burial had to be made as well. André Girard in his portrayal of the burial scene shows Father Damien lowering a deceased leper into a coffin, as Brother Dutton and others kneel to pray.

The next mural is particularly expressive because it depicts the disappointment of the lepers, when greatly needed provisions could not be delivered, and they realized the possibility of starvation. Girard portrays their skeletal figures in silhouette as they stand on the shore in attitudes of sheer frustration and anguish. In the distance they can see the boat that was to deliver the needed supplies getting farther away. Brother Dutton is seen rushing to the shore, while Father Damien follows quietly with his hands clasped in prayer.

In this third panel, Girard portrays Brother Dutton trying to complete the many plans and projects begun by Father Damien as well as trying to take care of the daily needs that required his attention. Some of the figures are shown surrounding Brother Dutton and waiting in line so he can assist them. Others are shown on their knees and reaching out to touch him to try to get his attention.

J—The Burial of Father Damien

His grave was dug in the cool shadow of the pandanus tree and around it the long line of mourners shuffled in sad and grotesque parade, clad in the pitiful paraphernalia of the burying associations he had founded. Their friend "Kamiano" was dead but they did not want to accept the mournful fact that he had gone and even when the grave was filled they refused to go. They sat on the ground, beating their breasts, swaying their bodies with misery, after the custom of their ancestors . . . p. 199 [34]

In portraying the death of Father Damien, Girard describes one of the saddest days for the leper colony. Father Damien had been the first person ever to give the lepers hope. He had taken care of them and given them dignity. He had shown them how to cope with their illnesses, and how to prepare for death. He was always there for them, as their most caring friend.

Girard creates a solemn setting by using a dominance of the color black in this composition. The vantage point of the viewer is different in this mural when compared to the others. André Girard does not portray the event as seen from a distance, but rather brings the viewer up close, directly behind the rows of lepers quietly mourning the loss of their beloved priest. Brother Dutton is shown silently praying beside the casket, accompanying Father Damien to the very end.

In the distance, we encounter figures in attitudes of unbridled frustration, showing their anger that Father Damien had been taken from them. Thus Girard expresses the full range of emotions that were brought about by Father Damien's passing. This makes the panel more compelling and touching to the viewer as they reflect on what the loss of Father Damien must have meant to his beloved congregation.

K—Brother Dutton Receives Recognition and Assistance

Another priest came to minister to the spiritual wants of the Colony; Sisters came to aid in the works but Dutton's work went on increasing. About this time Robert Louis Stevenson, the well-known author, came to visit Molokai and was shown about by Brother Dutton. Well-to-do business men in Honolulu, neither of whom was a Catholic, donated money for a boys' home and a girls' home, respectively. And when the United States Government took over the Islands, conditions improved still more. (From booklet on Brother Dutton written by Father McDonough.)[35]

The news of Father Damien's illness and death drew much attention to the selfless work he and Brother Dutton had been doing. In addition, it made known the tremendous need for assistance to be given in order to improve the difficult conditions that existed in the Colony. Fortunately, it also brought relief to Brother Dutton whose burdens had been ever increasing.

In this mural, Girard commemorates the arrival of the first nuns who came to Molokai. Brother Dutton is shown greeting the Franciscan Sisters, who came to assist him and Father Damien in their work. One has only to look at Brother Dutton's eager stride, his tightly clasped hands and the blissful expression on his face to understand what the arrival of the Sisters must have meant to him. Behind Brother Dutton, a few lepers are depicted bent over with cane in hand, coming to welcome their new caregivers. The nuns, under the guidance of Mother Marianne, (now St. Marianne) cluster together for moral support as they embark on this overwhelming new venture.

L—American Battleships Salute Brother Dutton

When in 1908, President Roosevelt sent sixteen battleships around the world, he learned that Brother Joseph earnestly hoped they might pass by Molokai. Immediately he wired the ships to go by the leper colony in battle formation. And so a grey-haired old man stood on shore, surrounded by his lepers, his hat on his breast and head erect while sixteen great ships of the United States Navy steamed slowly by and dipped their flags in salute to the aging veteran. (From booklet on Brother Dutton written by Father Mc-Donough.)[36]

As we complete our visual journey following Brother Dutton's life in Molokai, Girard presents us with a rendering of this historic moment which must have filled Brother Dutton's heart with pride and joy. Having served in the army and worked for the United States Government for many years, Dutton was very patriotic and proud of his American heritage.

André Girard depicts Brother Dutton and a few figures on the shore raising and saluting the American flag as was their daily custom. Suddenly they are transfixed by what they see in the distance—the silhouettes of the United States battleships precisely rendered, passing by in battle formation saluting Brother Dutton. The composition has a formal and ordered quality, suggesting a significant event is taking place. It illustrates an exceptional tribute by President Theodore Roosevelt and the United States Government for a man who had sacrificed his life in the service of others.

Blessed Sacrament Church before the doors and pediment were restored

RESTORATION OF THE DOORS AND PEDIMENT

The restoration of the murals on the façade of Blessed Sacrament Church presented Matthew H. Strong with his most difficult challenge. The paintings that André Girard had done on the doors no longer existed because the wood had deteriorated many years before and the doors had been replaced. The pediment, in turn, had been covered over with a new larger pediment in 2006 when the church was expanded to provide a narthex at the entrance.

Although I was able to provide Matthew with photographs of the restoration on the doors done in 1975, I did not have a clear picture of the restored pediment which had been difficult to photograph. The problem was that although the pediment received sunlight most of the day, the projecting eaves of the roof created deep dark shadows over the images. In addition to this, most photographs that had been taken by others were taken from a distance in order to fit the entire pediment in

one picture, and became blurred when enlarged. A good photograph of the pediment seemed not to exist. At this time Lynn Altadonna of the restoration committee came to the rescue. Through the Stowe Historical Society, he was able to locate an early black and white photograph of the front of the church that had the clarity and definition desired for the task ahead. Matthew and Lynn continued to work together in setting up the strategy of how to best proceed in the re-creation of the required images.

As Matthew described the process; "First, rolls of paper were cut to the exact size of the pediment. These papers were then taped in the desired position, to the wall of a large conference hall. Using Lynn Altadonna's computer, the photographic images were then digitized and projected onto the papers until they reached the exact size required for the pediment. The projected images could then be drawn on the papers."

Matthew H. Strong as he traces the images on to the pediment

Matthew then took over the process. He attached the tracings to the actual pediment with carbon papers behind them. In that way, he was able to transfer the images onto the wood.

Once this was done and corrections were made, the mural was ready to be painted using 1 Shot Sign Painters' Black.

Matthew explained this was a difficult task because the projections were not very clear. Since the pixels of the digital images were square, it made the images appear as if one was viewing them through a screen door.

Despite this difficulty, Matthew applied the paint to the unsealed wood, working as carefully as possible in order to follow the original artwork, using the photographs as well as the projected images. After the paint had dried, the mural was ready to be sealed with Marine Spar Varnish in hopes that it would be a stronger protection against the rays of the sun. This was then slightly sanded and the final coat applied was of a satin spar varnish to keep the glare off the surface. Matthew Strong's restoration of the paintings on the pediment and doors of the church was highly successful despite the fact that the original works no longer existed. Through hard work, dedication and ingenuity he was able to re-create Girard's original vision. The culmination of Girard's artistic narrative of Brother Dutton and Father Damien is to be found on the doors and pediment of

Blessed Sacrament Church. At first glance the paintings might seem to represent two separate scenes, but it is actually one painting expressing a singular concept.

In the lower part of the pediment André Girard represents the lepers of Molokai fervently looking towards heaven. Brother Dutton, and (now) Saint Damien, who are depicted in the upper part of the pediment, are shown guiding their flock to eternal glory. The Holy Spirit, symbolized by a beautiful flying dove, is shown soaring above them in the heavens.

The pediment is not the complete painting. Originally, the figures on the doors continued upward to join those in the pediment. However, when the church was expanded this upper section of the doors was replaced by glass panels in order to give more light to the vestibule. The figures on the doors represent the congregation and visitors to the church to whom Brother Dutton and St. Damien extend an invitation to follow them to eternal salvation.

Thus André Girard expresses the concept that Brother Dutton and Saint Damien were not only an inspiration to the people of their own time and place, but they are still a means of inspiring future generations to follow their lead and live lives characterized by generosity, love and caring for others. The mural is an extraordinary composition filled with meaning and spiritual significance.

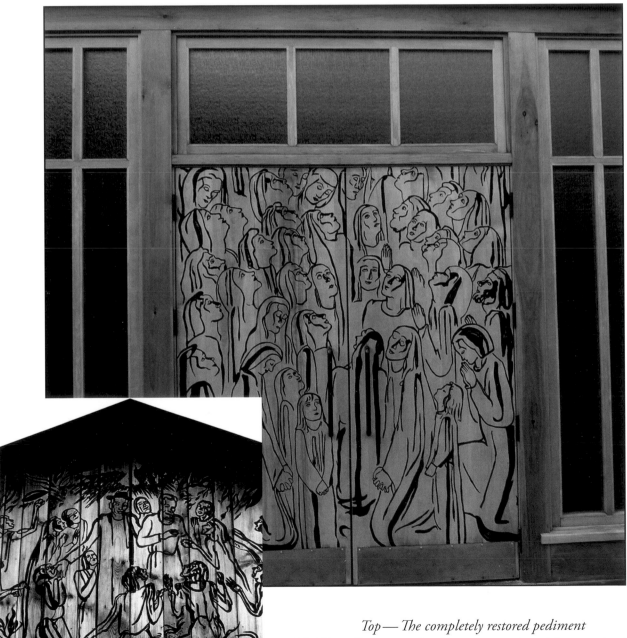

Top — The completely restored pediment
Middle — Figures on the doors representing visitors to the church
Left — The peak of the pediment with Brother Dutton, Father Damien,
their congregation and the Holy Spirit as a dove extending his blessings

63

BLESSED SACRAMENT CHURCH

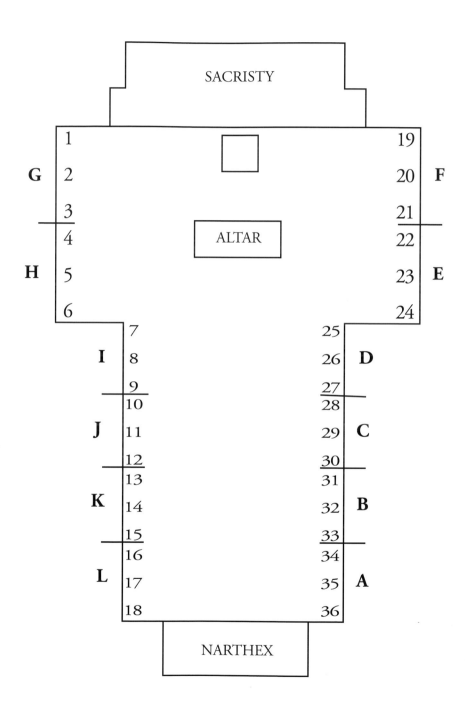

PEDIMENT AND DOORS

The Twelve Murals

A — Brother Dutton Meets Father Damien in Molokai

B — Father Damien Introduces Brother Dutton to the Lepers

C — Father Damien & Brother Dutton Working among the Lepers

D — Brother Dutton Assisting Father Damien at Mass

E — The Distribution of Holy Communion

F — Father Damien in the Confessional

G — The Burial of the Dead

H — Anguished Lepers Witness the Loss of Supplies

I — Brother Dutton Takes Over Additional Responsibilities

J — The Burial of Father Damien

K — Brother Dutton Receives Recognition and Assistance

L — American Battleships Salute Brother Dutton

Murals on West Elevation

2013: Blessed Sacrament Church after all restorations were completed

REFLECTIONS

by Matthew H. Strong

It was a crisp, clear morning in late summer when I put tools to the wood panels to start on my odyssey of restoring 12 murals on the Blessed Sacrament Church. I have spent months in research trying to get photos of the original paintings to no avail. The research on paints and varnishes had yielded what I thought would get the most durable final products. I had no idea how much the technique I had in mind would change by the end of the restoration, or how much more my own understanding and appreciation for the artwork and for the men in the story that the artwork was about, would change as well. As I worked on the peeling varnish, two women stopped to talk and asked about what I was doing. This turned out to be the providence of God as one of the women, Sr. Joy, said she had done some of the sanding of the murals herself, when her teacher had done a major restoration of the artwork at Blessed Sacrament in the early 1970s. Fortunately, Sr. Joy was able to get me in contact with her teacher, Josephine Belloso, who had studied under André Girard, himself.

Her knowledge and resources of photos were invaluable to me in bringing the paintings back as close as possible to their original form. The process of restoring the paintings ended up taking over 4 summers. The paint and varnish I used changed as I learned what did and did not work. To my surprise, I was told by a member of the Restoration Committee at Blessed Sacrament that a secondary restoration of the murals had taken place in 1994 and that the second restorer had chemically removed the original paint from the murals.

Therefore, my process went from trying to save what I thought was original paint to scraping down the whole panel and starting over with the image left on the wall from weathering and using photos from the past. Through my working on the restoration I gained an insight into what Girard intended to convey through the paintings. To most of us, the paintings are rather unusual and to some extent disturbing. This is as it was meant to be, for it portrays the sacrifice that Father Damien and Joseph Dutton made for the sake of those who suffered from leprosy. If one takes the time to look at the paintings and lets the story and the message come through, it is clear that the sacrifice is not glamorous, but the eternal glory brought about by that sacrifice outshines anything here on earth. I am truly richer in spirit from having had the honor and privilege of being part of the restoration of the artwork on the outside of the Blessed Sacrament Church here in Stowe, Vermont.

Collage of the windows relating to the Passion and Resurrection of Christ

DIGITAL RESTORATION AND PRESERVATION OF THE WINDOWS 2010–2013

VERMONT REVISITED

After 60 years the ravages of time and tempest took their toll on the paintings André Girard had done on the windows of Blessed Sacrament Church. It was inevitable—the extremes in temperature; and the sun, snow, sleet, and rain would create unsustainable conditions for the paintings to survive intact. By 2010, extreme deterioration had taken place, suggesting immediate action should be taken to preserve the windows, or they might reach a state beyond repair. The parish had considered several artists for the restoration, but although their painting was skillful, in their trial efforts they had been unable to recreate the unique painting style of André Girard. The parish council had wished to consult with me about this matter, but they no longer had a record of my address or telephone number since I had moved.

Fortunately, Joy Pellegrino, the former student who had visited me in Stowe in 1974 was traveling throughout New England. Close to the Vermont border, Joy, who is now a Sister of Charity, couldn't resist visiting Blessed Sacrament Church to see how the paintings were surviving. By speaking with Matt Strong, who was working on the exterior murals, Joy was asked if she could provide contact information in order to reach me.

Since I had done the earlier restoration of the church and had taken some slide photos at that time, a member of the committee at Stowe called me soon after S. Joy's visit. He asked for recommendations about how to restore the windows. I provided detailed information as to the materials and processes I had used originally, and even offered to advise any artists they were considering.

Finally, I received a call asking the most important question: "What could possibly be done with the windows so they would not have to keep being restored?" It was a challenging question. The more I thought about it the more I realized that trying to restore the windows by repainting and blending the colors into the original artwork, was not going to solve the problem on a permanent basis.

Upon serious reflection, the solution suddenly occurred to me; since old photographs could now be restored digitally, then my slide images of the windows taken in 1975 could be restored, printed on plastic film, and adhered between two sealed pieces of glass. These could then replace the original windows, hopefully thus preserving both the image, and vibrant colors, from the ravages of sunlight, wind, and extremes of temperature.

During a subsequent phone call, when I presented my solution to the problem facing Blessed Sacrament, there was a long silence at the other end of the telephone. I realized I had suggested a rather unorthodox solution, but the committee member agreed to present my idea.

When I had done the first restoration, the sections of the windows where the paint had dried out from the heat of the sun, would get loose and get attached to the brush when the new paint was applied. Now, after 60 years of exposure to the sun's rays, if the same process was used even more of the original paint would be removed, further damaging Girard's original artwork.

Although I deeply regretted suggesting the original works by André Girard be removed, my solution assured the windows could be preserved in perpetuity. A DVD of the restored paintings could be created, saved, and used to recreate the exact images of the windows as they might be needed in the future. In this way the legacy of André Girard, and the heritage of Blessed Sacrament Church, could be enjoyed by future generations. Since the original paintings would no longer have to be restored by different artists, the integrity of Girard's work could best be preserved. It was a daring, unique, but permanent solution to the problem.

Following several phone calls requesting technical information, I decided to call my friend and colleague, S. Jean Dominici DeMaria, OP, PhD who had taught digital art for 30 years at Molloy College. She was

CONDITION OF THE WINDOWS IN 2010

The Flight into Egypt

Jesus and the Lepers

able to provide answers to the many computer-related questions being asked. Before long we were challenged to produce one of the windows, restored in the manner I had suggested that could be a suitable and permanent solution. We, of course, chose one of the easier windows to restore first, but yet one that would demonstrate what could be done. With the approval of the pastor, Father Benedict Kiely we were encouraged to continue with the rest of the thirty-six windows. S. Jean immediately employed her expertise to begin the restoration.

In her own words:

The images were brought into Photoshop by scanning each slide at 600 ppi (pixels/inch). The window dimensions were specified at approximately 39 × 27. To reduce the size of the file, I decided to limit each window to a workable file. Thus the dimensions (39 × 27) were divided by 3 and became 13 × 9. This was then divided by 2 allowing for a workable size of 6.5 × 4.5.

I chose 600 ppi because the 6.5 × 4.5 digital print would have to be scaled by 600% to fit the 39 × 27 area. The pixel size for the print would thus be 100 ppi which would prevent the image from appearing pixelated to the viewer.

Each slide was scanned at 6.5 × 4.5 with a resolution of 600 ppi.

The process utilized to create a rectangle from the windows that were photographed on an angle and appeared as trapezoids follows:

Since each scanned image was 6.5 × 4.5 and 600 ppi, there was a problem with images where the window was on an irregular angle to the slide. Noting that the window was

Jesus Wakens the Diciples

Jesus and the Pharisees

distorted, I remembered that Photoshop had a function for Distortion. To test the possibility, I selected the window out of its surroundings, then copied and pasted it on another layer, discarded the original and changed the canvas size back to 6.5 × 4.5. The window image retained its 600 ppi. I then reselected the window image, went to the menu item Edit > Transform > Distort. A box with anchor points surrounded the distorted image. I dragged each of the anchor points until the corners of the distorted window filled the 6.5 × 4.5 rectangle.

The Nativity required a great deal of detailed painting, a marvelous function available in Photoshop. Josephine applied her painting expertise and soon mastered this technique. However, the star required a geometric application that called for a shape path and a radial gradient fill. A white second shape path was overlaid to embellish the star.

This description explains the technical foundation for the work we were to do.

While S. Jean's main focus was on the technical aspects of the restoration, my role was to concentrate on the painterly aspects. This meant I had to learn to paint with a computer. I was a little intimidated at the prospect, but when S. Jean opened up Photoshop, I saw the endless variety of brushes of every size, shape and texture. Add in the limitless range of colors and tools to be used to perform many functions, and it was like entering an art supply heaven. It was enlightening and exciting for me to see so many possibilities. I began painting timidly at first under the guidance of S. Jean, but soon began to gain confidence as I realized the

Sister Jean and I reviewing our progress on the computer

skills in painting I had developed previously could be adapted to the new medium. Eventually I even began to enjoy painting with my digital brushes and paints.

It was a major challenge for me, painting on photographs that were often flawed in many ways, rather than an actual window. The overhang of the roof often created partial shadows on the original slides. The photographs also did not have the true colors because they might have been taken at a particular time of day. The oil colors in the photographs are different from computer colors, so the blending of these different tones was difficult. Also, the photographs of my previous restoration were taken at various stages of my work, before the restoration was completed.

Since I studied with André Girard and restored so many of his films I have developed an innate sensitivity to his artistry, and always make every effort to preserve the integrity of his style. In fact, my most important goal is to integrate and blend my work with Girard's painting to the point it will be difficult to decipher where his last stroke ends and mine begins. If you cannot find evidence of my work, it means I accomplished what I set out to do.

"Suffer the Little Children to Come unto Me"

EARLY STAGES OF THE RESTORATION

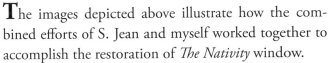

The First Stage   *The Second Stage*

The images depicted above illustrate how the combined efforts of S. Jean and myself worked together to accomplish the restoration of *The Nativity* window.

The first image of *The Nativity* shows the window in somewhat of the shape of a trapezoid because the slide was taken from below. S. Jean utilized the Photoshop distortion function to rectify the problem. She digitally removed the image from its surroundings, repositioned it on another layer, then discarded the original, and changed the canvas size to accommodate the true dimensions of the actual window. She then went to the Menu item edit>transform>distort. A box with anchor points surrounded the distorted image. She then dragged each of the anchor points until the shape was the required rectangular size.

In the second illustration I began to restore *The Nativity* window by filling in the empty spaces, using digital painting techniques. In the photograph of *The Nativity* the central areas which appear to be white were actually completely deteriorated, and devoid of paint. Every evening these same spaces would appear as black because the darkness of the night would be seen through the clear glass.

The result of this was the radiant star, the shepherd kneeling before the Christ Child, the Christ Child himself, and the faces of Mary and Joseph would completely disappear from view. During the day the brilliant sunlight would pass through the blank areas and draw attention to the central part of the painting which was not the true focal point.

By adding greater detail and modifying the contrast and intensity of the colors, greater definition and harmony was achieved. Therefore, attention was drawn to the right of the window, towards the figures of the Holy Family, just as André Girard had originally intended.

In the third illustration you can see I had deepened the richness of the colors and given greater definition to the faces and figures. By bathing each of the images in the Divine Light emanating from the Christ Child, it made them seem to glow against the darkness of the night, enhancing the beauty and dramatic impact of the scene.

In the fourth illustration S. Jean utilizes more of the geometric application to the star. This called for a shape path and radial gradient fill. A white second shape path was overlaid to embellish the star. These sequential images demonstrate how our combined skills made possible the restoration of Girard's striking and memorable painting.

The printing firm that achieved the greatest success in reproducing the artwork utilized a process which involved first printing on one side of vinyl sheeting, and then printing a translucent form of white on the back surface, followed by a printing of the reverse image on the white surface that would exactly match the first print. This not only illuminated the white tones, but the double sided printing intensified the brilliance of the colors. The placement of the second image was crucial, as the two needed to match to the finest degree of accuracy. The prints were made on Lintec, which is a transparent vinyl-based film with an adhesive paper backing. The photo image was first adhered to the thermal glass, and the paper film covering the adhesive was removed; then the entire glass was covered with a thin plastic film to protect the printed image.

Final Stages of the Restoration

The Third Stage

The Fourth Stage

After the printing firm had refined their process through trial and error, it was decided two of the restored windows at Stowe would be selected, printed, and mounted in place. A trial period encompassing all four seasons would allow for the effects of changes in weather, temperature, and sunlight to be studied and evaluated. A successful trial period allowed the project to move forward without delay. The congregation, noting the installation of the trial windows, expressed approval of the transformation that had given new life to the damaged windows.

André Girard's paintings on the windows of Blessed Sacrament Church are the culmination of his life-long, intense, and innovative experimentation of "painting on light". In the past Girard had painted on smaller glass panels but Blessed Sacrament Church, with its thirty-six continuous windows, provided a unique and extraordinary opportunity to more fully develop this painting technique. Girard was literally painting on light that was streaming through the windows as he produced these paintings. This added to the luminosity of the finished images and gave each work a spiritual dimension.

Upon entering the church most visitors are surprised by the darkness of its interior; however, this creates a feeling of being in an enclosure of sacred space. Once they look up they are almost blinded by a brilliant surge of color and light that sweeps around them, unfolding the sacred story of the life of Christ. The effect is truly amazing.

By the spring of 2013, all the windows were in place, and plans were being made for a May dedication and celebration. All past and present parishioners, donors, relatives, and friends were invited. S. Jean and I, of course, travelled to Stowe anxiously looking forward to seeing the fruits of our labors. We were not disappointed. The digitally restored images were wonderful to behold. After our morning lectures, which presented our restoration processes, we had the opportunity to meet with the parishioners and celebrate the artistic legacy of André Girard.

The highlight of our stay was when we received a most moving tribute from the pastor, Fr. Benedict Kiely. Blessed Sacrament Church was going to dedicate one of the windows to S. Jean and myself. Happily, they selected *The Transfiguration*, which was one of our favorites. It was hard to keep back the tears. The next morning before we left Stowe, I made a personal visit to the church to take one last look. The early morning sun was streaming through the windows that were glowing with color and light. After looking at each window, I reluctantly took my leave, taking with me many heartfelt memories.

Note: The following pages of this chapter show the differences between the restored and the un-restored windows, illustrating the life of Christ. The smaller photographs indicate their condition in 2010, before the restoration. The larger photographs show the windows after the restoration had been completed. Earlier slides were also used in the restorations.

Most of the windows have been arranged in sequencial manner, but in a few instances paintings have been grouped together to indicate their relevance to each other in expressing Christ's message. The number preceding the title of each painting indicates the actual sequence of its position in the church.

3—The Blessed Virgin as a Child

2—The Blessed Virgin among the Angels

4—The Annunciation

The windows facing west begin with André Girard's beautiful illustrations of the special graces and blessings bestowed on Mary by the angels, from the time of her childhood. A pious Mary is accompanied by exquisite celestial beings, with long, graceful gold-tipped wings. They surround her with a heavenly light. Girard portrays Mary, as she reaches maturity, with a radiant countenance to be acknowledged in the angel's greeting that addresses her as "filled with grace".

In Girard's painting of *The Annunciation*, as Mary accepts the angel's invitation, she is literally entrusted with God's Son. The window encompasses Girard's unique interpretation of the theme, with the manifestation of baby Jesus at this extraordinary biblical event.

Soft blue colors accented by shimmering white and gold highlights suggest the ethereal nature of God's messenger. The flowing movement of the angel's robe and wings convey a sense of its dynamic flight. The left side of the composition uses vibrant contrasting colors to draw attention to the significance of the event, in which the Second Person of the Blessed Trinity, like Mary, humbly accepted the will of His Father and took on a human form.

5—*The Nativity*

The birth of Christ was one of André Girard's favorite subjects. As a creative artist, he interpreted the theme in many ways, but always with a sense of awe and reverence for this sacred moment. *The Nativity* has a meditative and mystic quality. All is absolutely still. It is as if time has stopped and you have been blessed with an actual vision of the Christ Child's birth. We see the tenderness of Mary as she holds her newborn

close, the concern of Joseph as he prays beside her and the attitude of respect and veneration as the Magi and shepherds kneel in adoration of this Holy Child. The brilliant star that guided the Magi to Bethlehem pierces the midnight sky to illuminate every image, creating a transcendent quality to the scene before us.

In *The Flight Into Egypt*, André Girard's sparse and simple treatment conveys the challenges the Holy Family will be facing as they flee into Egypt to escape Herod's wrath. The fragile figures of Jesus, Mary and Joseph are silhouetted against a monumental pyramid and the stark, expansive desert they must cross to begin a new life. Girard introduces a whimsical touch by showing Joseph struggling to pull a rather reluctant donkey during this difficult journey.

After days of anguish because they had lost the young Jesus in Jerusalem, Mary and Joseph find Him in the temple with the doctors, asking them questions. Girard adds to the drama by creating a darkened setting with Jesus providing the enlightenment with His understanding of scripture.

6 — The Flight into Egypt

7—Jesus among the Doctors

8 — The Holy Family

Girard envisions the tranquil and grace-filled lives of the Holy Family in an idyllic setting. The soft, muted, purple tones of dusk permeate the entire scene. It is that peaceful, quiet time of the day when life proceeds at a slower pace. Mary attends to the Christ Child and St. Joseph, depicted as a strong and manly figure, turns to them with a caring, watchful gaze. As the foster father of Jesus, he would be the one responsible to guide and protect Him throughout His formative years. Girard depicts the interaction of the Holy Family in such a relaxed and natural way, that we can identify with them in terms of our own family relations. Children, as well, can identify with the young Jesus, who like them had to be under the care of His parents and be subject to them.

10—The Baptism of Jesus

St. John the Baptist was the last prophet to proclaim the coming of the Messiah to the Jewish people. Jesus acknowledges the significance of St. John's role in God's divine plan, by seeking to fulfill the saint's prophesy before beginning His own public life. André Girard emphasizes the humility of Jesus as He stands before St. John to be baptized, by depicting Him with head bowed and hands clasped in prayer.

Heightened drama is introduced by André Girard in his portrayal of the Holy Spirit, descending with magnificent outstretched wings, radiating His divine light. Simultaneously, God the Father makes His presence known by declaring this is His beloved Son in whom He is well pleased. Father, Son and Holy Spirit are revealed in this singular instant . . . a unique manifestation of the Triune God.

9—Jesus Tempted by the Devil

Before beginning His public ministry, Jesus prepared Himself by spending forty days and nights fasting in the desert. The devil knew Christ would be weak and vulnerable after this experience. Girard creates a glowing red radiance that accompanies the devil as he approaches Jesus. He offers Christ one of his most compelling appeals. If Christ will abandon the mission of His Father, which can only end with a painful death on the cross, the devil will reward Christ with all the pleasures, riches, and kingdoms of the world. An unusual feature of Girard's interpretation of the theme is that the devil is not portrayed as ugly or menacing, but rather as attractive, with twinkling eyes and an appealing smile. However, we have only to look at the rigid stance of Jesus, with tightly closed eyes and clasped hands, to know He has resisted the temptation and chosen to fulfill the mission of His Father.

Christ then begins His public life by gathering His first disciples and attending a wedding feast at Cana, where He performs His first miracle by changing water into wine, thus prefiguring the Eucharistic feast, when He would change bread and wine into His own body and blood.

12—Jesus with Andrew and John—the first Disciples

22—The Wedding Feast at Cana

25—Jesus and the Adulteress

14—"Suffer the Little Children to Come unto Me"

23—Jesus and the Woman at the Well

André Girard shows us that Jesus came into the world not only to bring salvation to those who were innocent, but also to forgive and transform sinners. This particular aspect of Christ's mission is graphically reflected in these three windows. When Christ is asked if an adulteress should be stoned to death, He begins writing in the sand, which seems to be aglow with the light of burning embers. In the story, as a protective gesture, Jesus asks her accusers if there is anyone who is without sin among them. Girard portrays them quickly disappearing into the distance, one behind the other; a revealing response to Christ's questioning challenge. Jesus then turns to the adulteress, does not condemn her, but tells her to go and sin no more.

In a similar instance, Girard illustrates Christ's encounter with the Samaritan woman at the well. Although knowing she is a sinner who has had five husbands, Christ's casual pose suggests He does not reject her, but rather invites her to change her life. Dominating the setting is a tree of impressive proportions with a beautifully textured bark and expansive branches. It extends itself over the figures, possibly alluding to the tree that provided Eve with the first temptation.

In *Suffer the Little Children to Come unto Me,* Girard presents us with a resplendent Christ, welcoming the children, who joyously run to be with Him. This is an unusual interpretation of the theme. The children are usually depicted as babies, but I believe André Girard was inspired to make them all little girls in contemporary dresses, because he had four lively daughters, whom he dearly loved. The painting is appealing and playful, and children viewing it will be happy to find Jesus loved them and had come for them, too.

15—Jesus Preaching to His Disciples

We know from the gospels Jesus invited many to follow Him, but He carefully chose the twelve apostles,

giving each of them a special calling. He kept them close to Him and offered them special explanations that would enlighten their understanding of scripture, the parables, and the meaning of His mission on earth.

André Girard captures the closeness of this relationship between the Master and His followers in the painting of *Jesus Preaching to His Disciples*. The time frame Girard chooses is early evening. They are gathered in what appears to be a grove of trees, as Jesus reveals to them the word of God. Although the apostles are informally posed, they have an attitude of rapt attention, trying to capture the nuance of every lesson He is passing on to them. A soft light emanates from Christ, reaching directly to each of them, symbolizing the divine aspect of His message.

13—Jesus Preaching among the Fishermen

Jesus often preached to the multitudes that followed Him wherever He went: whether to the mountains, the towns, or along the shores of the Sea of Galilee. In this painting André Girard depicts Christ preaching to the fishermen from one of their boats. It is the end of the day; the fishermen have returned their boats to the shore, but not yet taken down their sails. As Christ begins preaching, all movement stops, as they listen to His message. The vertical masts, the vivid sails, the violet coloring of the sky, are so effectively combined they create a unique interplay of rhythm, color and light. However, the eye is drawn to the radiant image of the Redeemer who stands out in His gleaming white robes.

17—Jesus and the Lepers

24—The Paralytic, "Take up thy bed and walk"

18—Jesus Calming the Disciples in the Boat

The Gospels record that Jesus performed many miracles. He cured physical ailments when He healed the wounds of the lepers, but He also came to cure man's spirit. Therefore, when He cured the paralytic, He also forgave him his sins.

There were certain miracles, however, that were specifically meant to be a revelation of Christ's divine nature. In the painting of *Jesus Calming the Disciples in the Boat*, Girard has summoned the full range of his own artistic potential to depict the limitless powers of the Son of God. The apostles, calmly fishing, suddenly find themselves in a perilous situation due to an approaching storm. The radiating flashes of glaring white light against the black sky suggest the intensity of the raging storm. The waters, moving in huge undulating waves, appear to be enveloping the small boat. As might be expected, the disciples are cowering in fear of the fate that awaits them. However, our eyes are drawn

to Jesus, calmly standing in the center of this whirling chaos. With a mighty gesture, He commands the powerful forces of nature to calm the storm. It is a riveting presentation that, despite its threatening aspect, has a sense of beauty in its artistic expression.

19—The Raising of Lazarus

11—The Sermon on the Mount

21—The Transfiguration

These events depicted are some of the most significant in the public life of Christ. Near the end of His public life Jesus takes Peter, James and John to a high mountain to pray. Suddenly, the apostles behold an extraordinary vision as Christ is transfigured before them. The apostles are astonished by this manifestation of Christ in His Divine Nature, as He is talking to Moses and Elijah. St. Matthew describes the face of Jesus as shining like the sun, and His garment as being white with light. Girard's interpretation of the *The Transfiguration* lives up to the superlative description by the evangelist. Jesus, Moses and Elijah all appear glorified wearing dazzling white garments, with an intense radiance of red, orange and yellow light being emitted from them. The profiles of the two apostles are shown as they witness this supernatural event.

When I did the first restoration of the windows in the church, I remember many visitors stopped at this window and became almost transfixed by its impact. I was often asked to explain its biblical reference.

André Girard portrays *The Sermon on the Mount* with illuminating rays representing the thoughts of Jesus, as He reveals to the multitudes the underlying principles of the Lord's kingdom. These were principles they were to follow as they lived out their lives.

The Raising of Lazarus from the dead prefigures Christ's own Resurrection. Girard's imagery is charged with pulsating energy, as Jesus stretches to reach down into what seems to be the netherworld, to literally pull Lazarus to the world of the living. The hands of Jesus and Lazarus do not yet touch. The anticipation of that moment gives the representation an added sense of action and excitement.

16—Jesus and the Pharisees

These images illustrate the beginning of Christ's journey to His Passion and the fulfillment of His mission on earth. The teachings of Jesus had most often been at odds with those of the Pharisees, who tried to discredit or trick Him at every opportunity. One such confrontational incident is presented here, with the Pharisees hiding in the darkness, as they plot against Him. Jesus points an accusing finger toward them as He continues to openly preach and spread the truth, enlightening all who hear Him.

At the Last Supper, we view the twelve apostles, seated at the table with Jesus as He institutes the Blessed Sacrament. At this significant occasion in the life of Christ and His Church, all the apostles are turned toward Him with an attitude of reverence and devotion. There is only one who looks away . . . the one who would betray Him.

After the Last Supper, Jesus invites His apostles to watch with Him while He goes to the garden to pray. André Girard depicts Christ bending close to awaken the apostles, and being disappointed to find them sleeping comfortably, completely unaware of the anguish He was facing.

26 — The Last Supper

28 — Jesus Wakes His Disciples

27—The Agony in the Garden

One of the most beautiful and moving windows at Blessed Sacrament Church is the rendering of *The Agony in the Garden*. André Girard presents us with a sensitive portrayal of a vulnerable Christ as He kneels to pray in an attitude of supplication. He is asking the Father if the cup of sacrifice cannot pass from Him, except He drinks it, then the Father's will be done. In contrast to the dark setting, dramatic flashes of deep red, orange, and white light heighten the drama and

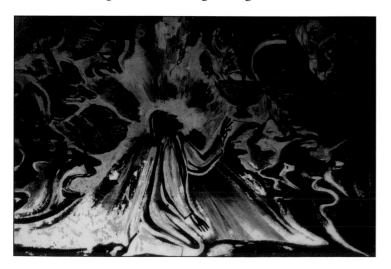

symbolize the pain Christ is experiencing. Even Christ's posture, with His head drawn into His raised shoulders, evokes an emotional response to His agony from those viewing the window. The artist surrounds Christ with a crowd of forceful tempters, urging Him to abandon His mission. In the end, despite the anguish, Jesus is seen courageously reaching up to drink from the cup, accepting the sacrifices. I remember this window also caused visitors to linger, and they seemed to take the time to reflect on its meaning.

The painting of *The Kiss of Judas* portrays a traitorous scene. Silhouetted against the moonlit sky, we see Jesus receiving the kiss of Judas, as His captors emerge from the darkness to arrest Him. The glowing light from Jesus reveals Judas, as well as his secretive conspirators in their clandestine efforts.

The next stage of Christ's Passion finds Him taunted and tortured by His accusers. A suffering Jesus, wearing a crown of thorns and a kingly robe, is surrounded by tormentors who ridicule and laugh at Him. Ironically, Christ is seated beneath the cross bearing the sign with which Pilate identified Him as King of the Jews.

29 — The Kiss of Judas

30 — The Mocking of Jesus

31—The Resurrection

In the interpretation of *The Resurrection*, Christ literally bursts forth from the tomb with an explosive power, impacting not only the stone covering the opening and the soldiers guarding the tomb, but the very atmosphere itself. The figure of Jesus, vigorous and strong, striding from the tomb, emits a powerful light that obliterates the darkness. He raises His arms in a mighty gesture, overcoming His own death and personifying His divine nature. Girard's vision inspires awe at the splendor of God's omnipotence, joy at His overcoming the sufferings of His crucifixion, and gratitude for His willingness to come to save us.

32—On the Road to Emmaus

In contrast to the dynamic impact of Girard's painting of Christ's Resurrection, we are now presented with a quiet, almost meditative scene. Two apostles come upon Jesus as they travel along a lonely road. The three are silhouetted against the dim light of dusk. It is a tranquil moment as Jesus speaks to them of the scriptures. The closeness of the apostles as they turn towards Christ indicates their desire to continue their journey with Him, in order to be further enlightened by His teachings. A mystical light seems to illuminate the road, and not only pass through the image of Christ, but also to emanate from Him.

20—Jesus Walking on the Waters

Girard illustrates this event from the point of view of the apostles in the boat. As they are out fishing, they see the vision of a mysterious form walking towards them on the water. The two apostles shown in the painting express surprise and apprehension in their gestures and the Bible states they actually feared the apparition might be a ghost. However, as Jesus comes closer to the boat, they begin to recognize Him. The warm radiance brought by Christ's presence encompasses the scene, giving it a supernatural quality. Girard uses an impressionistic style in this work, as can be observed by the interpretation of the water. His stippling technique is quite successful evoking the rippling effect of the waves near the shore. The use of varying depths of color, the application of textural effects, and the dramatic contrast of light and dark result in an arresting painting

33—Jesus Appears to His Disciples

After the Resurrection it was important for Jesus to appear in public in order to prove He had truly risen from the dead. This was especially important for the apostles because they were to be entrusted with spreading Christ's teachings. They would have to testify to His redemption and resurrection. André Girard allows us to witness an incident when Christ unexpectedly appears before the apostles, who have gathered in an upper room. The apostles look to the risen Lord with awe and reverence. It is possible the figure to the right might be St. Thomas, his hand outstretched to touch Christ, seeking proof of His true identity. A broad range of golden hues fills the room, evidencing Christ's divine nature.

35—Saint Paul

1—Apparition of the Blessed Virgin at LaSalette

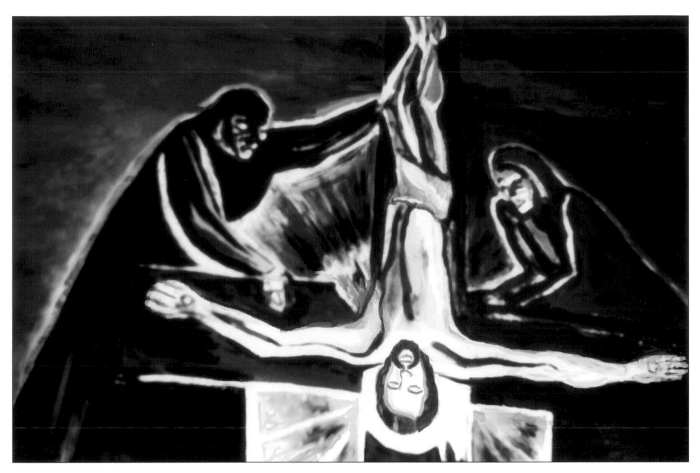

36—The Crucifixion of St. Peter

The themes at either extremity of Blessed Sacrament Church are not part of the life of Christ but relate to it. A dramatic illustration of the conversion of St. Paul shows such a compelling image of the crucified Christ, that it causes Paul to fall from his horse. The light radiating from Christ signifies not only His divinity, but also the illuminating grace by which Paul is drawn to conversion, resulting in the spreading of the faith to all corners of the earth. A loving, yet subtle, invitation is suggested by the way Christ is bending towards St. Paul; and Paul, although now blinded by this divine light, seems to be irresistibly drawn to it, completely transforming his life.

Apparition of the Blessed Virgin at LaSalette depicts the apparition of Mary, in the town of LaSalette, France. It reflects Girard's own piety and remembrance of his homeland devotions.

The Crucifixion of St. Peter illustrates how much the Saint had grown in faith and courage. In earlier times, St. Peter had denied Christ because of fear. Now we find him in a threatening situation, but glowing with grace. He not only accepts his fate to be crucified but insists on being crucified upside down, because he does not feel worthy to die in the same way as his Master.

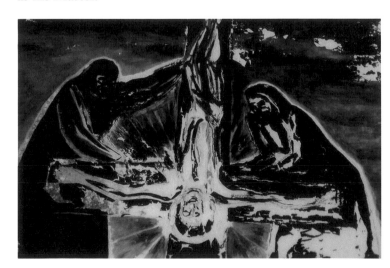

34—The Sacred Heart

Among the final windows on the east side of Blessed Sacrament Church is a rendering of the Sacred Heart of Jesus. Informal devotion to the heart of Christ had existed as far back as The Middle Ages. In the 17th Century, new impetus was given to the devotion by the apparitions of the Sacred Heart to St. Margaret Mary. In these visions Christ requested this devotion be spread. André Girard interprets this devotion with a creative vision of his own. Two pious supplicants humbly kneel on either side of a transcendent Christ who seems to be illuminated from a light within. With a benevolent gesture Christ unfolds His cloak to reveal His heart glowing with love. His desire to spread this love is symbolized by the red glow that emanates from Him, extending outwards to the whole world.

Collage of the windows of the public life of Christ

Blessed Sacrament Church

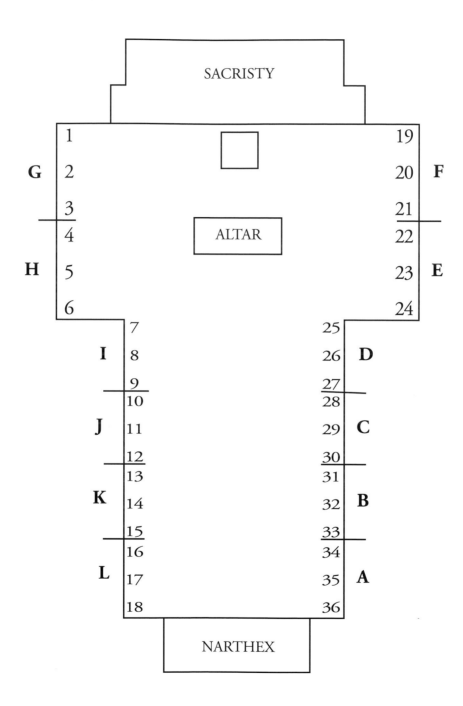

PEDIMENT AND DOORS

THE THIRTY-SIX WINDOWS

1—Apparition of the Blessed Virgin at LaSalette

2—The Blessed Virgin among the Angels

3—The Blessed Virgin as a Child

4—The Annunciation

5—The Nativity

6—The Flight into Egypt

7—Jesus among the Doctors

8—The Holy Family

9—Jesus Tempted by the Devil

10—The Baptism of Jesus

11—The Sermon on the Mount

12—Jesus with Andrew and John—the first Disciples

13—Jesus Preaching among the Fishermen

14—"Suffer the Little Children to Come unto Me."

15—Jesus Preaching to His Disciples

16—Jesus and the Pharisees

17—Jesus and the Lepers

18—Jesus Calming the Disciples in the Boat

19—The Raising of Lazarus

20—Jesus Walking on the Waters

21—The Transfiguration

22—The Wedding Feast at Cana

23—Jesus and the Woman at the Well

24—The Paralytic, "Take up thy bed and walk."

25—Jesus and the Adulteress

26—The Last Supper

27—The Agony in the Garden

28—Jesus Wakes His Disciples

29—The Kiss of Judas

30—The Mocking of Jesus

31—The Resurrection

32—On the Road to Emmaus

33—Jesus Appears to His Disciples

34—The Sacred Heart

35—St. Paul

36—The Crucifixion of St. Peter

Epilogue

Blessed Sacrament is a historic church. For several generations it has reflected the deep religious faith of its congregation and expressed pride in Stowe's heroic son, Brother Joseph Dutton. Through its restoration efforts, Blessed Sacrament has preserved an important aspect of Vermont's heritage and maintained the spirit of its own mission in a way that is still relevant and meaningful today.

The 36 windows André Girard painted at Blessed Sacrament Church in Stowe enabled him to utilize the full range of his creative artistry. The illustrations are compelling not only for their beauty but for the brilliant intensity with which they reveal Christ's story of mercy, forgiveness, and redemption.

Girard's virtuosity in the use of color is unparalleled. As the light passes through the windows, the richness of the colors seem to glow and they reflect throughout the church, creating an ethereal atmosphere. As you view each Biblical illustration, it draws you into its space. For a time, all other activity and distractions, including the other windows, seem to disappear as you reflect on its meaning. The image and the experience stays with you long after leaving, continuing to inspire.

André Girard continued his interpretation of God's message with the murals surrounding the church. His decision to illustrate the lives of Brother Dutton and Father Damien in epic proportions reflected his deep understanding of the significance of their lives of service. By vividly portraying their dedication as they brought hope and spiritual healing to the suffering and afflicted under their care, Girard created a memorable and enduring memorial for the world to witness and reflect upon. Since the murals have a strong visual impact they draw people's attention. Hopefully, those who stop to view them will be motivated to enter the church and discover the spiritual and artistic treasures within.

André Girard's artwork at Blessed Sacrament Church was really a far-sighted approach to church design and the creation of sacred space. It is extraordinary how the work he did has remained valid, during a time of so many liturgical changes. It has stood the test of time. Many visitors are amazed to find that the church is over 65 years old; they often think it is a new church, because of its unique approach and contemporary appearance. Blessed Sacrament is a jewel in the rough, a rustic wooden church suited to its time and place, beautiful and inspirational.

< *Detail of the Blessed Sacrament Altarpiece*

MEMORIAL STATUE OF IRA B. DUTTON

*Sacred Hearts Father William Petrie and friends posed with the new statue of Brother Joseph (Ira) Dutton
on the grounds of St. Joseph Church Kamalo, Molokai (photo courtesy of Catherine Cluett)*

A recent tribute to Ira B. Dutton has been the com-missioning of a seven-foot marble statue of young Dutton in his Civil War Army uniform. It is meant to honor Dutton's service to God and country and his fellow man. In an article published on July 22, 2013, by *The Molokai Dispatch*, Catherine Cluett reports that "Because of his status as a military veteran and the struggles he overcame he has become a role model and inspiration for some of our veterans today."[37]

It is hoped that the statue will be placed in Kalaupapa National Historic Park alongside the statues of Father Damien and Mother Marianne, but since it will take time to receive Federal approval, it has tempo-rarily been placed on the grounds of St. Joseph Church in Kamalo, Molokai. This happens to have been one of the early churches constructed by Father Damien him-self when he came to Hawaii.

On March 4, 2014, the House of Representatives 27th Legislature 2014 of the State of Hawaii h.c.r. NO. 73 passed the following House Concurrent Resolution: "Recognizing Captain Ira Barnes Dutton and urging the National Park Service to work toward relocating his statue from its current location at Saint Joseph Church in Kamalo to the Kalaupapa Peninsula . . . Be it further resolved that certified copies of this Concurrent Resolution be transmitted to the Secretary of the Interior, Director of the National Park Service, and Secretary of the United States Department of Veterans Affairs."[38]

The Resolution will need to be processed and approved by the Federal Legislature, but in the meantime it has the support of the state officials, the Hawaiian war veterans, and Ira Barnes Dutton's many friends and admirers.

A Dedicated Life Inspires a Call for Sainthood

Since Brother Joseph Dutton passed to his heavenly reward in 1931, there have been continuous calls to begin the process of his cause for sainthood. Both Father Joseph Damien who served the lepers for 16 years in Molokai, and Mother Marianne Cope who worked alongside Brother Dutton for 33 years, have recently been declared saints. Many believe Brother Dutton who spent 45 years ministering to the needs of the afflicted and who accomplished so much improving the conditions at the settlement, deserves at least a similar consideration.

A possible reason why Brother Dutton's case has not been established is that he was not a member of a religious order which would have devoted itself to sponsoring his cause. The citizens of Hawaii, however, have not abandoned this hope and after several years of persistent requests to the Diocese of Honolulu, it has begun to respond to their petitions.

The Hawaii Catholic Herald, which is the official newspaper of the Diocese of Honolulu, published an article on July 31, 2015 entitled "Layman, Soldier, Saint?" in which it states: "The Diocese of Honolulu has taken the first official step on the long and complicated road to the possible canonization of an American layman and civil war veteran who spent half his life serving leprosy patients."[39] It also states that "On June 23 Bishop Larry Silva approved the statute of the Joseph Dutton Guild charging it with the mission of spreading knowledge of, and devotion to, Ira 'Brother Joseph' Dutton as well as addressing the financial and logistical needs for his cause for sainthood."[40]

Although Brother Dutton lived between the nineteenth and twentieth centuries, his life was not unlike that of any individual today who is faced with struggles, temptations, and challenges of the contemporary world. Part of Dutton's life was far from perfect. Although he had an exemplary army career he became discouraged and depressed at the end of the Civil War, and turned to alcohol to forget his troubles. Pamela Young, in an article entitled "Brother Dutton A Candidate for Sainthood," published by *Maui Magazine*, presents an interesting theory about his behavior at this time. She reports that Maria Devera, a physician at Schofield Barracks Health Clinic had suggested that like many of today's returning veterans, Joseph Dutton might have been suffering from post traumatic stress disorder at that time. [41]

The redeeming factor of Dutton's life was that at the age of forty he realized he needed to end the destructive behavioral aspects of his life and completely transformed his outlook, focusing not on himself and his problems but on God and doing penance by helping others. Joseph Dutton was not a model of perfection, operating on a spiritual plane higher than those around him. He was an *everyman* striving to serve God as best he could. In fact, *The Hawaii Catholic Herald*, on April 25, 2014, published an article by Mary Adamski entitled "Saint Potential in Blue Denim," in which she states: "There's a small but growing group of people in Hawaii and elsewhere who envision a future Saint in blue denim . . ."[42]

People today might not be able to identify with some of the saints from the past who seemed to have led perfect lives and might even have experienced heavenly visions. They can, more easily, identify with Brother Dutton who had a penchant for communicating with others all over the world. His address book had about 4,000 names. They can understand Brother Dutton's struggles with life and be inspired by his spiritual transformation which led him to eventually become a person of heroic virtue, serving God and attending to the needs of the suffering humanity of his time.

Only time will tell whether Brother Joseph Dutton will ever achieve sainthood, but we can hope that one day he might be able to join in the good company of Saint Damien and Saint Marianne again, just as he had done in Molokai many years ago.

André Girard: Selected Index of

LITURGICAL ART IN CHURCHES AND UNIVERSITIES

St. Vincent Archabbey, Latrobe, Pennsylvania—triptych

1949—Blessed Sacrament Catholic Church, Stowe, Vermont—altarpiece, stations of the cross, ceiling, windows, exterior murals

1952—St. Ann's Chapel, Stanford University, Palo Alto, California—windows, stations of the cross

1955—Church of St. Anthony, Nepara Park, New York—windows

Marquette University Library, Milwaukee, Wisconsin—mural

ONE-MAN SHOWS

1923—Paris, Théâtre de L'Oeuvre
1929—Paris, Galerie Pleyel
1932—Paris, Galerie de l'Elysée
1934—Paris, Galerie de l'Elysée
1937—Geneva, Musée de l' Athénée
1938—New York, Cornelius Dullivan Gallery
1940—San Francisco, Art.Gallery
1944—New York, Bignou Gallery
1946—Paris, Galerie Bignou
1950—New York, Bignou Gallery
1951—Philadelphia, Art Alliance
1952—New York, Carstairs Gallery
1954—New York, Carstairs Gallery
1956—New York, Carstairs Gallery
1958—Houston, Bute Gallery
1960—Philadelphia, Art Alliance
1963—South Bend, Notre Dame University
1967—New York, Queensborough Community College
1973—Muncie (Ind.), Ball State University
1977—Paris, Galerie Helene Appel
1982—New York, Queensborough Community College

PAINTINGS IN THE FOLLOWING COLLECTIONS

Millicent Rogers (New York)
Otto Lucien Spaeth (New York)
Rev. Th. Pitcairn (Philadelphia)
André Pacatte (Virginia)
Sonnin Krebs (Wilmington)
Pierre Monteux (Hancock, Maine)
Mr. & Mrs. Bjorkman (Paris)
Presidential Collection, Queensborough Community College, (Bayside, New York)
Mrs. Ed. Hudson (Houston, Texas)
Dr. Robert Wallis (New York)
Mr. & Mrs. L. H. Eldredge (San Francisco)
Miss Ruth M. O'Neill (New York)
Mrs. Clare Booth Luce (New York)
Atelier André Girard
7, rue Campagne Premiér
75014 Paris France

COLLECTION OF PRINTS

Professor Josephine Belloso (New York)

ADDITIONAL CREATIVE ACHIEVEMENTS

Illustrated books for the Limited Editions of the Societe du Livre d' Art in France before World War II

Represented in the permanent collections at the French State Museum and the Museé Athénée of Geneva as well as elsewhere in Europe and America

Paintings exhibited in group shows at the Whitney Museum, New York, and the Dayton, Milwaukee, Houston and Fort Wayne Museums.

Executed frescoes in several pavilions of the Paris International Exposition, 1937

Director of the French Pavilion at the San Francisco World's Fair, 1938; executed several murals for the Fair

Executed several murals for the French Pavilion at New York World's Fair, 1940

HAND PRINTED BOOKS

(Limited ,Editions)
LITHOGRAPHY
(date unknown)—*The Raven* by Edgar Allan Poe
1937—*L'Autre Monde* (The Other World), by Cyrano de Bergerac
SERIGRAPHY
1949—*Heraclite d' Ephèse* (The Sayings of Heraclitus). 125 pages, 50 copies.
1950—*Le Chemin de Croix* (The Stations of the Cross). 14 pages, 50 copies.
1950—*Paul Verlaine: Poesie Diversies* (Poems of Verlaine). 64 pages, 50 copies.
1951—*Mon Coeur Mis a Nu* (My Heart Laid Bare) by Charles Baudelaire. 80 pages, 30 copies. 1951—*O Terre Detresse* (O Land of Anguish) by Lucienne Laurentie.
1951—*Sonnets*—by Jean Pierre Bauer.
1956—*The Sayings of Jesus.* 120 pages, 60 copies.

WRITINGS PUBLISHED

1944—*Bataille Secrete en France*, Book published and reprinted in *Reader's Digest*.
1944–1945—Series of articles published in *Town & Country*.
1961–1962—Several articles publsihed in *The Critic*

A pen and ink drawing by André Girard for a section of the film, "The Raven," based on the poem by Edgar Allan Poe

WORKS, EXHIBITS AND HONORS[43]

STAGE DESIGNS

1921—*Le Partage de Midi* by Paul Claudel, designed for Madame Lara

—*Measure for Measure* by William Shakespeare and *Liliom* by Molnar for Pitoeff

1923—*La Gioconda* from Gabriele D'Annunzio for Lugne Poe

Additional stage designs included

Ce Soir on Improvise by Pirandello

La Ronde by Schnitzler for Pitoeff

Halte on Allez Vous? by Gerber for Lugne Poe.

HAND-PAINTED FILMS

(Transferred to 16 mm)

Note: André Girard began painting films in 1959, and continued to produce them through 1968.

The Story of Abraham (82 min.)

Berceuse and Jardin de Dolly (5 min.)

Patrick Will Take Over, Story and narration by William Ready (26 min.)

Homage to Venice and Claude Debussy (15 min.)

The Tell Tale Heart by Edgar Allan Poe (20min.)

The Life of Jesus

Part I—The Nativity, narrated by Peter Ustinov (25 min.)

Part II—The Sermon on the Mount (35 min.)

Part III—Miracles and Parables (38 min.)

Part V—Passion and Resurrection (47 min.)

The above films are in the collection of the Queensborough Community College Library.

FILM PRESENTATIONS

1969—Lincoln Center, Alice Tully Hall, New York City, "Unique Show of Films Painted on Light by André Girard." A presentation of five films.

1972—Concert performance ofan Oratorio, "The Story of Abraham," by Richard Yardumian in close synchronization with the Girard film. Performed at Albert Hall, London, as well as Philadelphia, Knoxville, Muncie, and other cities.

1975—Presentation for the critics of all the films by Girard, at the Cinema of Arts, "Les Ursulines," Paris.

ADDITIONAL FILMS

Edgar Allan Poe's poems—

To F.S.O.—The Haunted Place—The Conqueror Worm—A Dream in A Dream—For Annie—Eldorado—To the River—The Bells—Zante (27 min.)

The Raven—Annabel Lee (18 min.)

The Trip to the Moon and to the Sun by Cyrano de Bergerac (90 min.)

The Life of Jesus—Part IV "The Last Commandment" (45 min.)

La Fille Aux Cheveux De Lin—Gollywog's Cake Walk by Claude Debussy—Played by Gaby Casadesus (8 min.)

English Proverbs Part II—Selected by Stephane Mallanne (12 min.)

Les Djinns by Victor Hugo—narrated by Robert Manuel de La Comedie Fram;aise (5 min.)

The Song of Songs from The Bible (18 min.)

Nuages et Fêtes by Claude Debussy—directed by Pierre Monteux (15 min.)

Minstrels by Claude Debussy—played by Gaby Casadesus (3 min.)

English Proverbs, selected by Stephane Mallarme—Part I (12 min.)

Mallarme's Short Poems (14 min.)

Arabesque—La Serenade Interrompue played by Gaby Casadesus (8 min.)

LaFontaine's Most Famous Fables

TELEVISION PRESENTATIONS

1957—"Look Up and Live," oil paintings of the "Sermon on the Mount," CBS.

1958—"Lamp Unto My Feet," oil paintings of the "Passion and Resurrection," CBS.

1959—"Hallmark Christmas Festival," hand painted 70mm film, *The Nativity*, NBC.

1959—*The Sermon on the Mount and the Passion and Resurrection*, hand painted 70 mm films, CBS.

1962—"Cabeza de Vaca," Cantata by George Antheil, illustrated by André Girard, CBS.

1969—*Le Girard Que Je Propose*, a commemorative one-hour presentation on the life and work of André Girard, CBS.

1977—Four programs of Girard films, including the *Passion and Resurrection* were shown on television in France as well as Canada.

HONORS RECEIVED

1948—Awarded the Legion of Merit by President Harry S. Truman for his distinguished service to the United States as a liaison officer of the French Underground Movement during World War II.

1958—Awarded the honorary degree of Doctor of Letters by Marquette University

1959—Received the Television Arts Award given by the National Council of Catholic Men

1962—Awarded Distinguished Contribution to the Arts by The Catholic Fine Arts Society

REFERENCES

1. McDonough, Rev. Francis E. "A Reminiscence", in *Brother Joseph Dutton 1843–1931 A Saint for Vermont.* Edited by Richard Halpern 1981. Stowe, Vermont. Blessed Sacrament Catholic Church. p. 16.

2. Ibid. pp. 16–17

3. Ibid. p. 18.

4. Ibid. p. 19.

5. Ibid. p. 18.

6. DeVolder, Jan. Translated by John Stephen. 2010. *The Spirit of Father Damien the Leper Priest—A Saint for Our Times.* San Francisco, California. Ignatius Press. pp. 113–114.

7. Ibid. p. 142.

8. Crouch, Howard E. and Sister Mary Augustine SMSM. 1981. *After Damien Dutton.* Damien Dutton Society for Leprosy Aid. Belmore, New York. p. 110.

9. Case, Howard D. ed. 1931. *Joseph Dutton His Memoirs.* Honolulu: Honolulu Star Bulletin Ltd. p. 203.

10. Ibid. p. 203.

11. Skinsnes, Anwei V. 1981. "A Self-Imposed Exile: The Life of Brother Joseph Dutton 1843–1931," in *A Saint For Vermont.* ed. By Richard Halpern, Stowe, Vermont p. 2, quoting Brother Joseph Dutton as cited by Crawford White in "Heroic Worker Among the Lepers." Human Life, Oct. 1907.

12. Ibid. p. 2 as quoted in "Calvin Coolidge Says." *McClure Newspaper Syndicate.* 1931.

13. von Trapp, Maria Augusta, 1959. *A Family on Wheels.* Philadelphia and New York. Lippincott Co. p 171

14. Bunson, Margaret and Matthew Bunson. 2009. *Apostle of the Exiled St. Damien of Molokai.* Huntington, Indiana. Our Sunday Visitor Publishing Division, Our Sunday Visitor Inc. p. 80.

15. DeVolder, Jan. *The Spirit of Father Damien.* p. 44.

16. Skinsnes, Anwei V. "A Self-Imposed Exile," p. 9, quoting Warren G. Harding as cited by Charles J. Dutton in *The Samaritans of Molokai.* New York Dodd, Mead & Co. 1932. p. 179.

17. Ibid., p. 9. quoting Franklin D. Roosevelt as cited by the Archives of St. Jude's Church, Beloit, Wisconsin. p. 193.

18. DeVolder, Jan. *The Spirit of Father Damien.* p. 112.

19. Skinsnes, Anwei V. "A Self-Imposed Exile," p. 8 as recorded by Emma Warren Gibson. *Under the Cliffs of Molokai.* Fresno, Academy Library Guild, 1959. p. 47.

20. Ibid. p. 6 Letter from Father Damien to Fr. Hudson, 1886, as cited in Br. Joseph Dutton File, Rev. David E. Hudson Papers, University of Notre Dame Archives. Notre Dame, Indiana.

21. Ibid. p. 6 as written by A.A. Mouritz in *The Path of the Destroyer*. Honolulu. Honolulu Star Bulletin Ltd. 1916 pp. 285–286.

22. Case, Howard D. ed. 1931. *Joseph Dutton His Memoirs*. p. 10.

23. Ibid., p. 242.

24. Girard, André. 1961. "An Artist in the Holy Land," *The Critic*, vol x14. no. 5.

25. Belloso, Josephine. ed. 1982. *André Girard: Modern Master*. Bayside, New York. Queensborough Community College. p. 42.

26. Scott, Aurelia Grether. 1982. "In My Father's House Are Many Mansions," in *André Girard: Modern Master*. p. 5.

27. Farrow, John. 1937. *Damien the Leper*. Franklin, Wisconsin, Sheed and Ward. p. 179.

28. Ibid. p. 180.

29. Ibid p. 180.

30. Ibid. p. 181.

31. Ibid. p. 119.

32. Ibid. p. 120.

33. Ibid. p. 186.

34. Ibid. p. 199.

35. McDonough, Rev. Francis E. Booklet on *Brother Joseph Dutton*. Stowe, Vermont. Blessed Sacrament Catholic Church.

36. Ibid.

37. Cluett, Catherine. *The Molokai Dispatch*. Molokai, Hawaii. July 22, 2013.

38. The House of Representatives 27th Legislature 2014 of the State of Hawaii h.e.r. N073. March 4, 2014.

39. "Layman, Soldier, Saint?". *Hawaii Catholic Herald*, July 31, 2014.

40. Ibid. June 23, 2015.

41. Young, Pamela, "Brother Dutton: A Candidate for Sainthood," *Maui Magazine*, Maui, Hawaii.

42. Adamski, Mary. "Saint Potential in Blue Denim," *Hawaii Catholic Herald*. April 25, 2014.

43. Belloso, Josephine. ed. 1982. *André Girard, Modern Master*. Bayside, New York. Queensborough Community College, p. 46.

Credits for Photography and Illustrations

The following authors, publishers and individuals were the sources of the images used throughout the book.

Altadonna, Lynn. Blessed Sacrament parishioner.
   Matthew H. Strong restoring a mural, p. 51
   Matt reproducing details, p. 52
   Matt tracing images of the pediment, p. 54

Archives of St. Joseph's College, Brooklyn, New York.
   André Girard at an exhibition, p. 20

Belloso, Josephine.ed. 1982 *André Girard: Modern Master*, Bayside, New York,
   Queensborough Community College
   Pen and ink drawing for a film sequence:
   "The Raven" by Edgar Allen Poe, pp. 108–109

Blessed Sacrament Catholic Church Directory Life Touch.
   Rev. Benedict Kiely, p. v

Bunson, Margaret and Matthew Bunson. 2009 *Apostle of the Exiled Saint Damien of
   Molokai.* Huntington, Indiana. Our Sunday Visitor Publishing Division, Our
   Sunday Visitor.
   Fr. Damien with a few choir members, p. 12

Case, Howard D.ed. 1931 "Joseph Dutton His Memoirs." Honolulu: *Honolulu Star-
   Bulletin* Ltd.
   Ira B. Dutton in his Civil War uniform, p. 11
   Br. Dutton in front of his cottage, p. 13
   Br. Dutton seated outside of his office, p. 16
   Photo sent to friends, p. 16

Cluett, Catherine. 2013. *The Molokai Dispatch*, Molokai, Hawaii
   Marble statue of Ira B. Dutton, p. 106

Costa, Joseph. 1962 Photographs originally appeared in "Painting on Light". *New York
   Mirror Magazine,* King Features Syndicate Inc.
   Girard painting on 70mm film, p. 28
   Scene from the Crucifixion, p. 28
   Scene from the Resurrection, p. 29
   Girard with specially built projector, p. 29

Crouch, Howard E. and Sister Mary Augustine SMSM. 1981. *After Damien Dutton*
   originally published by the Damien Dutton Society for Leprosy Aid. Bellmore,
   New York
   Gethsemani Monastery, p. 11

Br. Dutton with Fr. Damien's horse Daisy, p. 12
St. Philomena Church, p. 14
Br. Dutton taking down the American flag, p. 16
Ships from the Great White Fleet, p. 15

Damien Dutton Call 1977. Damien Dutton Society for Leprosy Aid, Inc. Bellmore, New York.
Sketch of Father Joseph Damien by Edward Clifford

DeBelloso, Isabel. 1975.
Restoration of the pediment in progress, p. 44
Splitting the scaffold to reach the extremities, p. 46

DeVolder, Jan. Translated by John Steven. 2010. *The Spirit of Father Damien the Leper Priest—A Saint for Our Times*. San Francisco, California. Ignatius Press. Used by permission.
Father Damien lying in state, p. 13

McMurray, Jeanne. 2013
The twelve outdoor murals of Brother Joseph Dutton and Father Damien in Molokai pp. 50–60

Morrissey, Jack, Blessed Sacrament Parishioner. 1975.
Restoring a window, p. 36
The sanding process, p. 39
Applying the glaze to the doors, p. 43

Skinsness, Anwei V. 1931. "A Self-Imposed Exile: The Life of Brother Joseph Dutton." in *Brother Joseph Dutton—A Saint for Vermont*. Richard Halpern ed. Stowe, Vermont.
Raising and saluting the flag, p. 15
Br. Dutton and boys from the Baldwin Home, p. 14

Stowe Free Library. Stowe, Vermont
Blessed Sacrament Catholic Church 1949. Photo by Richard Garrison, pg.3
Br. Joseph Dutton, p. vii
Br. Joseph Dutton 1828, p. 10

von Trapp, Maria Augusta. 1959 *A Family on Wheels*. Philadelphia and New York.
Lippincott Co., p. 171
The Trapp Family Singers at the grave of Br. Dutton, p. 17

Willis, Eloise. 1975
Painting above the boiler, p. 42
Completing the pediment restoration, p. 47
Josephine Belloso, p. 114
Sister Jean DeMaria O.P., p. 115
Matthew Strong, p. 115

Most of the photographs not credited above were taken by the author.

The serigraph prints reproduced in the chapter on André Girard are from the collection of the author as well.

ARTISTS PARTICIPATING IN THE RESTORATION PROCESS

JOSEPHINE BELLOSO
Author

A Professor Emeritus of St. Joseph's College in New York, Josephine Belloso has been a professional artist as well as a teacher. She has received numerous commissions, some of which include: the 14 Stations of the Cross, carved in wood for St. Paul's Abbey in Newton, New Jersey, as well as an eight foot relief sculpture of St. Benedict for the entrance of their monastery church. She also created a nine-foot relief sculpture of the Holy Family for the façade of the Dillon Child Study Center of St. Joseph College.

Additional commissions include a three-foot Madonna of Redemption carved in wood for St. Gabriel's Monastery in Pennsylvania as well as a bronze portrait bust of her grandfather, Dr. Lucio Oquendo, for an outdoor plaza in San Cristobal, Venezuela. Her bronze portrait bust of André Girard is with the collection of his works at his Atelier in Paris, France. She edited a book about André Girard, published by Queensborough Community College in New York, and restored five of his hand-painted 70 mm films on the life of Christ, as well as Girard's last film, *The Story of Abraham.*

Further commissions: a portrait of Msgr. Martin O'Dea for Holy Family Parish; a statue of St. Francis Xavier Cabrini for The Catholic Alumni Club of NYC; and a relief sculpture of The Holy Family, commissioned by the faculty of Marymount Manhattan College for the departure of Sr. Edmund Harvey, RSHM, former Dean.

Throughout her career, Ms. Belloso was named Artist in Residence at Marywood College in Scranton, Pennsylvania as well as at Queensborough Community College in New York, where she was also appointed Curator for the Retrospective André Girard Art Exhibition and Film Festival in 1982. She has received several national awards for her religious sculptures from Paul VI Institute of the Arts in Washington, D.C. As an educator, she most enjoyed the adventure of taking students throughout Italy, England, France and Spain to study the Art and Architecture of Western Europe.

**King of Kings
Lord of Mercy**

Sculpture by
Josephine Belloso
given to
Blessed Sacrament Catholic Church
2017

Sister Jean Dominici DeMaria, OP is a Dominican Sister (Amityville, NY), who has been engaged in education from elementary through high school and college levels. Her specialty in art and art education expanded to digital art subsequent to her doctoral studies at NYU. Her PhD dissertation (1991) addressed the phenomenological analysis of the works of Charles Csuri, a computer artist and art educator at Ohio State University. Csuri was later acclaimed as the Father of Computer Art.

Now a Professor Emerita at Molloy College, she also achieved Artist-in-Residence status at Marywood College (1985 and 1993) when she shared her expertise as a digital artist.

Her professional background includes: Secretary-Treasurer, and President for the Catholic Fine Arts Society and also CEO of the Catholic Artists of America. In addition, she was a Board of Trustee member for the National Museum of Catholic Art and History, serving on the Art Advisory Committee and Secretary of the Executive Board. She served on the Board of Directors for the LI Arts Council at Freeport and was elected as Vice-President and later Treasurer.

Sister Jean has exhibited her work extensively from 1981 through 2008. In addition, she continues to work as a free-lance digital artist.

Matthew H. Strong was born in Craftsbury Common, Vermont in 1957. Given a pocketknife at the age of eight to help him with his farm chores, in his spare time, he was soon carving wooden spoons and miniature figures. Mathew has continued to develop these natural talents through his work in the design, construction and fine arts woodworking fields. His carvings not only adorn unique niches and panels of homes, but often tell a story. For example, in a Vermont home where he did the carving of a mermaid as a masthead figure on the prow of a sailing ship, or in a New Hampshire estate where he was commissioned to carve a dragon as well as gargoyle motifs.

Matthew has done reproduction carvings for the Church of St. Vincent Ferrer in New York City. This entailed matching the carvings of moldings in the early 1900s style for a handicap entryway. He also did carvings for a baptismal font for the Grace Lutheran Church in Chicago. Annually, he carves graduation canes for a senior society at Dartmouth College in New Hampshire.

A resident of Stowe, Vermont, Matthew teaches carving classes throughout the state and has private students as well. Currently, he is president of the Green Mountain Wood Carver's Association.

INDEX

Diagrams designating the location of murals and windows can be found on pages 64–65 and 102–103.